Inspired Quotes
from the Pen
of
Shakespeare

Compiled by:

Deanne M. Muir
Kayleen M. Scott
Marie Wahlquist

Illustrations by:

Ken Jensen

4th Printing, October 1991

ISBN 0-9630987-0-5

Printed by Publishers Press

Copyright © 1991 Deanne M. Muir
P.O. Box 1451, Ogden, UT 84402

Thinkest thou to copy one page? Do not...The Bard will haunt thee in thy cell.

This book we dedicate to all speakers, students, and teachers who want to quote the wisdom of Shakespeare during sermons, lectures, or discussions; and have always wished for a fast way to find the perfect passage.

We also dedicate this book to our families. May they find ". . . joy and enlightenment in these pages."

". . . good phrases are surely, and ever were, very commendable."
King Henry IV, Part II (III, ii)

FOREWORD

You are listening to some guy talk and he comes up with some bit of wisdom that sounds right, inspired even. "Heavy," you say. "Shakespeare," he says. "Forsooth," you say and you go away thinking, "This guy doesn't sleep like the rest of us. He stays up all night reading Shakespeare so he can find the precise quote worded in such a way that the meaning jumps out in 'some delightful ostententation!' " (Love's Labour's Lost V.i)

Well, now you don't have to stay up all night reading Shakespeare to find those perfect epigrams. These three lovers of the wit and wisdom of the Bard have stayed up all night for you. The quotes have been arranged by topic and play in alphabetical order to make them easy to find. Some topics include quotes of opposite meaning, i.e., the subject of injustice might be found under the heading of justice. Each quotation is used only once, though it may relate to more than one topic.

So you keep this book close to your other source books: scriptures, thesaurus, yellow pages (this one will get used too); and the next time a salesman says, "What time is it?" you reply, " 'Time to be honest,' (pause) Timon of Athens, act I, scene i."

The next day you are in a business meeting or faculty meeting, and as it stretches overtime you rise and walk out saying, " 'I have important business, the tide wherof is now,' Troilus and Cressida, act V, scene i."

And husbands, here is a real time-saver. "Pardon me, wife: henceforth do what thou wilt." (Merry Wives of Windsor IV.iv)

Great uses! For church sermons, for motivational seminars, for dates (you get nervous not knowing what to talk about when you remember, "...twixt such friends as we/ Few words suffice," Taming of the Shrew I.ii), for a thought for the day ("But heaven hath a hand in these events," King Richard the Second V.ii), for teachers ("Hell is empty and all the devils are here," The Tempest I.ii), for birthdays ("tis age that nourisheth," Taming of the Shrew II.i), for students ("Shake off this downy sleep, death's counterfeit...," Macbeth II.iii), or just for your own meditation and introspection ("Thou turn'st mine eyes into my very soul...," Hamlet III.iv).

In Deanne's copy of the complete works of Shakespeare, on the inside front cover, I scribbled these words which are also appropriate in this forword: "May you find joy and enlightenment in these pages and pass this on that our family be blessed.

"Not being able always to verbalize wisdom from the Fount of Wisdom (deity), we learn and drink from the writings of those who do."

FERRIL R. MUIR

CONTENTS

ADVERSITY	1
ANGER	6
BIBLE PEOPLE & PLACES	8
CHARACTER	11
CHARITY	15
CHOICES	17
COMMITMENT	19
COMMUNICATION	21
CONSCIENCE	24
CONSEQUENCE	28
CONTENTION	30
COUNTENANCE	32
COURAGE	34
DEATH	36
DEBT	39
DEITY	40
DEPRESSION	41
DEVIL	42
EARTHLY PROBATION	43
FAITH	48
FAMILY	49
FLATTERY	53
FORGIVENESS	54
FRIENDSHIP	56
GOSSIP	59
GRATITUDE	62
GREED	65
HEALTH	68
HONESTY	70
HONOR	73
HOPE	75
HUMILITY	76
HYPOCRISY	78
IMMORTALITY	87
INFLUENCE	89
INNOCENCE	91
JUDGMENT	92

CONTENTS

JUSTICE	94
KINDNESS	98
KNOWLEDGE	99
LAW	101
LEADERSHIP	102
LOVE	105
LOYALTY	110
LUST	112
MARRIAGE	114
MERCY	116
MORALITY	117
MUSIC	119
OBEDIENCE	121
PARENTING	122
PATIENCE	123
PRAYER	125
PREPARATION	127
PRIDE	128
RECORD KEEPING	130
REPENTANCE	131
REPUTATION	135
SELF-CONTROL	136
SELFISHNESS	138
SERVICE	139
SIN	141
SORROW	145
TEMPTATION	149
TIME	151
TOLERANCE	153
TRUST	154
TRUTH	155
VALUE	156
VIRTUE	157
WAR	160
WEALTH	164
WISDOM	165
WORK	167

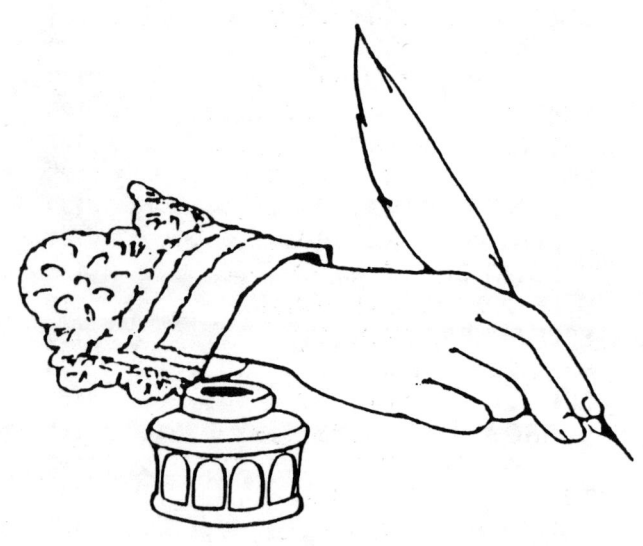

"... such virtue hath my pen..."
Sonnet LXXXI

ADVERSITY

                     . . . as the icy fang
And churlish chiding of the winter's wind,—
Which, when it bites and blows upon my body,
Even till I shrink with cold, I smile, and say. . .
These are counsellors. . .
Sweet are the uses of adversity. . .
And this our life. . .
Finds tongues in trees, books in the running brooks,
Sermons in stones, and good in every thing.
                As You Like It (II, i)

...but mountains may be removed with earthquakes...
                As You Like It (III, ii)

I had rather have a fool to make me merry than experience to make me sad. . .
                As You Like It (IV, i)

                  You were used
To say extremity was the trier of spirits,
That common chances common men could bear,
That when the sea was calm all boats alike
Showed mastership in floating.
                Coriolanus (IV, i)

                  . . . yet famine,
Ere clean it o'erthrow nature, makes it valiant.
Plenty, and peace, breeds cowards; hardness ever
Of hardiness is mother.
                Cymbeline (III, vi)

                  Come; our stomachs
Will make what's homely, savoury: weariness
Can snore upon the flint, when resty sloth
Finds the down pillow hard.
                Cymbeline (III, vi)

ADVERSITY

I have the patience to endure it now.
Even so great men great losses should endure.
Julius Caesar (IV, iii)

. . . Turning past evils to advantages.
King Henry IV, Part II (IV, iv)

Will fortune never come with both hands full. . .
She either gives a stomach, and no food.—
Such are the poor in health; or else a feast,
And takes away the stomach,—such are the rich,
That have abundance, and enjoy it not.
King Henry IV, Part II (IV, iv)

There is some soul of goodness in things evil,
Would men observingly distil it out;
For our bad neighbour makes us early stirrers,
Which is both healthful, and good husbandry;
Besides, they are our outward consciences,
And preachers to us all; admonishing,
That we should dress us fairly for our end;
Thus may we gather honey from the weed,
And make a moral of the devil himself. . .
'Tis good for men to love their present pains. . .
King Henry V (IV, i)

Thus sometimes hath the brightest day a cloud;
And after summer evermore succeeds
Barren winter, with his wrathful nipping cold.
So cares and joys abound, as seasons fleet.
King Henry VI, Part II (II, iv)

Oh, sir, to willful men
The injuries that they themselves procure
Must be their schoolmasters.
King Lear (II, iv)

ADVERSITY

When we our betters see bearing our woes,
We scarcely think our miseries our foes.
        King Lear (III, vi)

Henceforth I'll bear affliction till it do cry out itself,
"Enough, enough," and die.
        King Lear (IV, vi)

Bettering thy loss makes the bad-causer worse...
        King Richard III (IV, iv)

              ... those
That would make good of bad and friends of foes!
        Macbeth (II, iv)

              I am one...
Whom the vile blows and buffets of the world
Have so incensed that I am reckless what
I do to spite the world.
        Macbeth (III, i)

Let there be some more test made of my metal
Before so noble and so great a figure
Be stamped upon it.
        Measure for Measure (I, i)

All difficulties are but easy when they are known.
        Measure for Measure (IV, ii)

Then let us teach our trial patience...
        Midsummer Night's Dream (I, i)

I'll show you those in troubles reign,
Losing a mite, a mountain gain.
        Pericles (II, i)

ADVERSITY

He puts on sackcloth, and to sea. He bears
A tempest, which his mortal vessel tears,
And yet he rides it out.
     Pericles (IV, iv)

Adversity's sweet milk, philosophy,
To comfort thee. . .
     Romeo and Juliet (III, iii)

. . . all these woes shall serve
For sweet discourses in our time to come.
    Romeo and Juliet (III, v)

Or call it winter, which being full of care,   *[rare.*
Makes summer's welcome thrice more wish'd, more
    Sonnet LVI

I saw him beat the surges under him,
And ride upon their backs. He trod the water,
Whose enmity he flung aside, and breasted
The surge most swoln that met him. His bold head
'Bove the contentious waves he kept, and oared
Himself with his good arms in lusty stroke
To the shore, that o'er his wave-worn basis bow'd,
He came alive to land.
     The Tempest (II, i)

Do not, for one repulse, forego the purpose
That you resolv'd to effect.
    The Tempest (III, iii)

    All thy vexations
Were but my trials of thy love, and thou
Hast strangely stood the test: here, afore Heaven,
I ratify this my rich gift.
    The Tempest (IV, i)

ADVERSITY

All torment, trouble, wonder, and amazement
Inhabits here: some heavenly power guide us
Out of this fearful country!
           The Tempest (V, i)

Poet: How goes the world?
Painter: It wears, sir, as it grows.
           Timon of Athens (I, i)

And in some sort these wants of mine are crowned,
That I account them blessings...
           Timon of Athens (II, ii)

He's truly valiant that can wisely suffer
The worst that man can breathe...
           Timon of Athens (III, v)

           Why then, you Princes,
Do you with cheeks abash'd behold our works;
And call them shames, which are indeed naught else
But the protractive trials of great Jove,
To find persistive constancy in men?
The fineness of which metal is not found
In Fortune's love; for then the bold and coward,
The wise and fool, the artist and unread,
The hard and soft, seem all affin'd and kin:
But, in the wind and tempest of her frown,
Distinction with a broad and powerful fan,
Puffing at all, winnows the light away;
And what hath mass or matter, by itself
Lies rich in virtue and unmingled.
           Troilus and Cressida (I, iii)

ANGER

Counsel may stop a while what will not stay;
For when we rage, advice is often seen
By blunting us to make our wits more keen.
           A Lover's Complaint (stanza 23)

           . . . never anger
Made good guard for itself.
           Antony and Cleopatra (IV, i)

Put not your . . . rage into your tongue.
           Coriolanus (III, i)

           Pray be counseled,
I have a heart as little apt as yours,
But yet a brain that leads my use of anger
To better vantage.
           Coriolanus (III, ii)

Anger's my meat. I sup upon myself. . .
           Coriolanus (IV, ii)

           Anger is like
A full-hot horse, who being allowed his way,
Self-mettle tires him.
           King Henry VIII (I, i)

Heat not a furnace for your foe so hot
That it do singe yourself.
           King Henry VIII (I, i)

           . . . is woe the cure for woe?
Do wounds help wounds, or grief help grievous deed?
Is it revenge to give thyself a blow? . . .
Such childish humour from weak minds proceeds.
           Lucrece (stanza 261)

ANGER

Isabella: Oh, I will to him and pluck out his eyes!
Vincentio: This nor hurts him nor profits you a jot.
Forbear it therefore, give your cause to
Heaven.
Measure for Measure (IV, iii)

The brain may devise laws for the blood, but a hot temper leaps o'er a cold decree.
Merchant of Venice (I, ii)

He will fence with his own shadow.
Merchant of Venice (I, ii)

. . . dart not scornful glances from those eyes. . .
It blots thy beauty as frosts do bite the meads. . .
Taming of the Shrew (V, ii)

A woman moved is like a fountain troubled,
Muddy, ill-seeming, thick, bereft of beauty;
And while it is so, none so dry or thirsty
Will deign to sip or touch one drop of it.
Taming of the Shrew (V, ii)

To be in anger is impiety. . .
Timon of Athens (III, v)

BIBLE
PEOPLE & PLACES

. . . it out-herods Herod; pray you, avoid it.
Hamlet (III, ii)

Clown: There is no ancient gentlemen but gardeners, ditchers, and grave-makers; they hold up Adam's profession.
Clown: Was he a gentleman?
Clown: He was the first that ever bore arms.
Clown: Why, he had none.
Clown: What, art a heathen? How dost thou understand the scripture? The scripture says, Adam digged; could he dig without arms?
Hamlet (V, i)

[fields,
As far as to the sepulchre of Christ . . . in those holy
Over whose acres walk'd those blessed feet,
Which, fourteen hundred years ago, were nail'd
For our advantage, on the bitter cross.
King Henry IV, Part I (I, i)

...thou knowest, in the state of innocency, Adam fell...
King Henry IV, Part I (III, iii)

. . . as ragged as Lazarus in the painted cloth, where the glutton's dogs licked his sores . . . that you would think, that I had a hundred and fifty tattered prodigals, lately come from swine-keeping, from eating draff and husks.
King Henry IV, Part I (IV, ii)

I am as poor as Job, my lord, but not so patient. . .
King Henry IV, Part II (I, ii)

BIBLE
PEOPLE & PLACES

Your naked infants spitted upon pikes,
Whiles the mad mothers with their howls confus'd
Do break the clouds, as did the wives of Jewry,
At Herod's bloody-hunting slaughtermen.
             King Henry V (III, iii)

To say the truth, so Judas kiss'd his master,
And cried—<u>all hail</u>! whenas he meant—all harm.
             King Henry VI, Part III (V, vii)

And stand securely on their battlements,
As in a theatre, whence they gape and point
At your industrious scenes and acts of death. . .
Do like the mutines of Jerusalem. . .
             King John (II, ii)

Which blood, like sacrificing Abel's, cries,
Even from the tongueless caverns of the earth. . .
             King Richard II (I, i)

Three Judases, each one thrice worse than Judas!
             King Richard II (III, ii)

Disorder, horror, fear, and mutiny,
Shall here inhabit, and this land be call'd
The field of Golgotha, and dead men's sculls.
             King Richard II (IV, i)

Did they not sometime cry, <u>all hail</u>! to me?
So Judas did to Christ; but he, in twelve,   [none
Found truth in all but one; I, in twelve thousand,
             King Richard II (IV, i)

BIBLE
PEOPLE & PLACES

Though some of you, with Pilate, wash your hands,
Showing an outward pity; yet you Pilates
Have here deliver'd me to my sour cross,
And water cannot wash away your sin.
          King Richard II (IV, i)

As thoughts of things divine,—are intermix'd
With scruples, and do set the word itself
Against the word.
As thus,—<u>Come, little ones</u>; and then again,—
<u>*It is as hard to come, as for a camel*</u>
<u>*To thread the postern of a needle's eye.*</u>
          King Richard II (V, v)

With Cain go wander through the shades of night,
And never show thy head by day nor light.
          King Richard II (V, v)

How fain, like Pilate, would I wash my hands
Of this most grievous guilty murder done!
          King Richard III (I, iv)

A kissing traitor!—How art thou prov'd Judas?
          Love's Labour's Lost

. . . Adam's sons are my brethren. . .
          Much Ado About Nothing (II, i)

. . . since Noah was a sailor.
          Twelfth Night (III, ii)

CHARACTER

Sir, I am a true labourer; I earn that I eat, get that I wear; owe no man hate, envy no man's happiness; glad of other men's good...
As You Like It (III, ii)

Oh, that you could turn your eyes toward the napes of your necks and make but an interior survey of your good selves! Oh, that you could!
Coriolanus (II, i)

*It is held
That valor is the chiefest virtue and
Most dignifies the haver.*
Coriolanus (II, ii)

He's the rock, the oak not to be wind-shaken.
Coriolanus (V, ii)

*To shame the guise o' the world, I will begin
The fashion,—less without and more within.*
Cymbeline (V, i)

*... I never saw...
Such precious deeds in one that promis'd nought
But beggary and poor looks.*
Cymbeline (V, v)

*... he was too good, to be
Where ill men were; and was the best of all
Amongst the rar'st of good ones...*
Cymbeline (V, v)

*It shows a will most incorrect to heaven;
A heart unfortified, a mind impatient;
An understanding simple and unschool'd...*
Hamlet (I, ii)

CHARACTER

Assume a virtue, if you have it not.
That monster, Custom, who all sense doth eat,
Of habits evil, is angel yet in this,—
That to the use of actions fair and good
He likewise gives a frock or livery,
That aptly is put on. Refrain to-night,
And that shall lend a kind of easiness
To the next abstinence: the next more easy;
For use almost can change the stamp of nature,
And master the devil, or throw him out
With wondrous potency.
                  Hamlet (III, iv)

. . . for the eye sees not itself
But by reflection, by some other things.
                Julius Caesar (I, ii)

His life was gentle, and the elements
So mixed in him that Nature might stand up
And say to all the world, "This was a man."
                Julius Caesar (V, v)

Defect of manners, want of government,
Pride, haughtiness, opinion, and disdain;
The least of which, haunting a nobleman,
Loseth men's hearts, and leaves behind a stain
Upon the beauty of all parts besides,
Beguiling them of commendation.
                King Henry IV, Part I (III, i)

My lord, 'tis but a base ignoble mind
That mounts no higher than a bird can soar.
                King Henry VI, Part II (II, i)

CHARACTER

And I had twenty times so many foes,
And each of them had twenty times their power,
All these could not procure me any scathe,
So long as I am loyal, true, and crimeless.
            King Henry VI, Part II (II, iv)

Be great in act, as you have been in thought.
            King John (V, i)

I do profess to be no less than I seem—to serve him truly that will put me in trust, to love him that is honest, to converse with him that is wise and says little, to fear judgment, to fight when I cannot choose.
. .

            King Lear (I, iv)

            Obey thy parents, keep thy word justly, swear not . . . set not thy sweet heart on proud array.
            King Lear (III, iv)

Know thou this, that men
Are as the time is.
            King Lear (V, iii)

            Music do I hear?
Ha, ha! keep time!—How sour sweet music is,
When time is broke, and no proportion kept!
So it is in the music of men's lives.
            King Richard II (V, v)

God bless thee, and put meekness in thy breast,
Love, charity, obedience, and true duty!
            King Richard III (II, ii)

CHARACTER

The king-becoming graces—
As justice, verity, temperance, stableness,
Bounty, perseverance, mercy, lowliness,
Devotion, patience, courage, fortitude—
Macbeth (IV, iii)

One that, above all other strifes, contended especially
to know himself.
Measure for Measure (III, ii)

Opinion's but a fool, that makes us scan
The outward habit by the inward man.
Pericles (II, ii)

. . . for we are gentlemen,
That neither in our hearts nor outward eyes,
Envy the great nor do the low despise.
Pericles (II, iii)

I hold it ever,
Virtue and cunning were endowments greater
Than nobleness and riches: careless heirs
May the two latter darken and expend;
But immortality attends the former,
Making a man a god.
Pericles (III, ii)

. . . to be valiant is to stand.
Romeo and Juliet (I, i)

How use doth breed a habit in a man!
Two Gentlemen of Verona (V, iv)

CHARITY

And do not seek to take your change upon you,
To bear your griefs yourself, and leave me out;
For, by this heaven, now at our sorrows pale,
Say what thou canst, I'll go along with thee.
            As You Like It (I, iii)

How bitter a thing it is to look into happiness through
another man's eyes!
            As You Like It (V, ii)

A wretched soul, bruised with adversity,
We bid be quiet when we hear it cry;
But were we burdened with like weight of pain,
As much, or more, we should ourselves complain.
            Comedy of Errors (II, i)

. . . for to the noble mind
Rich gifts wax poor when givers prove unkind.
            Hamlet (III, i)

Deliver all with charity.
            King Henry VIII (I, ii)

Love thyself last. Cherish those hearts that hate thee.
            King Henry VIII (III, ii)

. . . that comfort comes too late.
'Tis like a pardon after execution.
            King Henry VIII (IV, ii)

In sooth, I would you were a little sick,
That I might sit all night, and watch with you. . .
And with my hand, at midnight held your head;
Still and anon cheer'd up the heavy time. . .
            King John (IV, i)

CHARITY

Gloucester: Now Good sir, what are you? [blows,
Edgar: A most poor man, made tame to fortune's
Who, by the art of known and feeling sorrows,
Am pregnant to good pity.
King Lear (IV, vi)

And who can sever love from charity?
Love's Labour's Lost (IV, iii)

So play the foolish throngs with one that swoons,
Come all to help him, and so stop the air
By which he should revive.
Measure for Measure (II, iv)

He jests at scars that never felt a wound
Romeo and Juliet (II, ii)

O, I have suffer'd with those that I saw suffer.
The Tempest (I, ii)

The truth you speak doth lack some gentleness,
And time to speak it in; you rub the sore,
When you should bring the plaster.
The Tempest (II, i)

Every man shift for all the rest, and let no man take
care for himself. . .
The Tempest (V, i)

For pity is the virtue of the law,
And none but tyrants use it cruelly.
Timon of Athens (III, v)

CHOICES

A man is master of his liberty.
Comedy of Errors (II, i)

In debating which was best, we shall part with neither.
Comedy of Errors (III, i)

You are at point to lose your liberties.
Coriolanus (III, i)

Determine on some course
More than a wild exposture to each chance
That starts i' the way before thee.
Coriolanus (IV, i)

Men at some time are masters of their fates.
The fault, dear Brutus, is not in our stars,
But in ourselves, that we are underlings.
Julius Caesar (I, ii)

Between the acting of a dreadful thing
And the first motions, all the interim is
Like a phantasma or a hideous dream.
The Genius and the mortal instruments
Are then in council, and the state of man,
Like to a little kingdom, suffers then
The nature of an insurrection.
Julius Caesar (II, i)

There is a tide in the affairs of men
Which taken at the flood leads on to fortune;
Omitted, all the voyage of their life
Is bound in shallows and in miseries.
. . . we must take the current when it serves,
Or lose our ventures.
Julius Caesar (IV, iii)

CHOICES

Let go thy hold when a great wheel runs down a hill, lest it break thy neck with following it, but the great one that goes up the hill, let him draw thee after.
 King Lear (II, iv)

*The art of our necessities is strange,
That can make vile things precious.*
 King Lear (III, ii)

*Oh, I do fear thee, Claudio, and I quake
Lest thou a feverous life shouldst entertain,
And six or seven winters more respect
Than a perpetual honor.*
 Measure for Measure (III, i)

Provost: I am your free dependant.
 Measure for Measure (IV, iii)

Our bodies are our gardens; to the which our wills are gardeners: so that if we will plant nettles, or sow lettuce; set hyssop, and weed up thyme; supply it with one gender of herbs, or distract it with many; either to have it sterile with idleness, or manured with industry; why, the power and corrigible authority of this lies in our wills.
 Othello (I, iii)

. . . there's small choice in rotten apples.
 Taming of the Shrew (I, i)

COMMITMENT

[duty.
King: Farewell; and let your haste commend your
Cour: In that and all things will we show our duty.
Hamlet (I, ii)

Now bid me run,
And I will strive with things impossible...
Julius Caesar (II, i)

I should not urge thy duty past thy might—
Julius Caesar (IV, iii)

I am fresh of spirit and resolved
To meet all perils very constantly.
Julius Caesar (V, i)

And in devotion spend my latter days,
To sin's rebuke, and my Creator's praise.
King Henry VI, Part III (IV, vi)

If we shall stand still
In fear our notion will be mocked or carped at,
We should take root here where we sit...
King Henry VIII (I, ii)

Oh, Cromwell, Cromwell!
Had I but served my God with half the zeal
I served my King, he would not in mine age
Have left me naked to mine enemies.
King Henry VIII (III, ii)

And the conjunction of our inward souls
Married in league, coupled and link'd together
With all religious strength of sacred vows...
It is religion that doth make vows kept...
King John (III, i)

COMMITMENT

I am tied to the stake, and I must stand the course.
King Lear (III, vii)

. . . My state
Stands on me to defend, not to debate.
King Lear (V, i)

. . . the duty that you owe to God. . .
King Richard II (I, iii)

My heart this covenant makes, my hand thus seals it.
King Richard II (II, iii)

. . . be the same in thine own act and valor
As thou art in desire?
Macbeth (I, vii)

. . . never anything can be amiss,
When simpleness and duty tender it.
Midsummer Night's Dream (V, i)

A gentleman . . . that loves to hear himself talk, and will speak more in a minute than he will stand to in a month.
Romeo and Juliet (II, iv)

COMMUNICATION

What's amiss, may it be gently heard; when we debate
Our trivial difference loud, we do commit
Murder in healing wounds: then, noble partners,—
The rather, for I earnestly beseech,—
Touch you the sourest points with sweetest terms...
            Antony and Cleopatra (II, ii)

... learn to jest in good time.
There's a time for all things.
            Comedy of Errors (II, ii)

Unquiet meals make ill digestions.
            Comedy of Errors (V, i)

Do not cry havoc where you should but hunt
With modest warrant.
            Coriolanus (III, i)

Give every man thine ear, but few thy voice...
            Hamlet (I, iii)

... brevity is the soul of wit...
            Hamlet (II, ii)

            O, speak to me no more!
These words, like daggers, enter in mine ears...
            Hamlet (III, iv)

            [strokes...
Words before blows...good words are better than bad
            Julius Caesar (V, i)

And yet, words are no deeds.
            King Henry VIII (III, ii)

Ill-will never said well.
            King Henry V (III, vii)

COMMUNICATION

A man may see how this world goes with no eyes.
Look with thine ears.
>*King Lear (IV, vi)*

>*Her voice was ever soft,*
Gentle and low, an excellent thing in woman.
>*King Lear (V, iii)*

O, but they say, the tongues of dying men,
Enforce attention, like deep harmony;
Where words are scarce, they are seldom spent in vain
For they breathe truth, that breathe their words in
>pain.
>*King Richard II (II, i)*

O, sir, 'tis better to be brief than tedious. . .
>*King Richard III (I, iv)*

Why should calamity be full of words? . . .
Windy attorneys to their client woes,
Airy succeeders of intestate joys,
Poor breathing orators of miseries!
Let them have scope; though what they do impart
Help not at all, yet do they ease the heart.
>*King Richard III (IV, iv)*

How every fool can play upon the word! I think the best grace of wit will shortly turn into silence, and discourse grow commendable in none only but parrots.
>*Merchant of Venice (III, v)*

>*Note this before my notes,*
There's not a note of mine that's worth the noting.
>*Much Ado About Nothing (II, iii)*

COMMUNICATION

Sure, sure, such carping is not commendable...
But who dare tell her so? If I should speak,
She would mock me into air; O, she would laugh me
Out of myself, press me to death with wit.
     Much Ado About Nothing (III, i)

Celestial as thou art, O, pardon, love this wrong.
To sing the heavens' praise w' such an earthly tongue.
     Passionate Pilgrim (III) &
     Love's Labour's Lost (IV, ii)

Confusion's cure lives not in these confusions.
     Romeo and Juliet (IV, v)

I will be brief, for my short date of breath
Is not so long as is a tedious tale.
     Romeo and Juliet (V, iii)

These words are razors to my wounded heart.
     Titus Andronicus (I, i)

Thou know'st no less but all; I have unclasp'd
To thee the book even of my secret soul.
     Twelfth Night (I, iv)

       [with them.
Words are grown so false, I am loth to prove reason
     Twelfth Night (III, i)

Let me hear from thee by letters . . . what news. . .
Betideth here in absence of thy friend;
And I likewise will visit thee with mine.
     Two Gentlemen of Verona (I, i)

That man that hath a tongue, I say, is no man,
If with his tongue he cannot win a woman.
     Two Gentlemen of Verona (III, i)

CONSCIENCE

The heaviness and guilt within my bosom
Takes off my manhood...
Knighthoods and honours borne
As I wear mine, are titles but of scorn.
            Cymbeline (V, ii)

O, 'tis too true!   *[conscience*
How smart a lash that speech doth give my
The harlot's cheek, beautied with plast'ring art,
Is not more ugly to the thing that helps it,
Than is my deed to my most painted word:
O, heavy burden!
            Hamlet (III, i)

Thou turn'st mine eyes into my very soul;
And there I see such black and grained spots...
            Hamlet (III, iv)

To my sick soul, as sin's true nature is,
Each toy seems prologue to some great amiss:
So full of artless jealousy is guilt,
It spills itself in fearing to be spilt.
            Hamlet (IV, v)

Suspicion always haunts the guilty mind;
The thief doth fear each bush an officer.
            King Henry VI, Part III (V, vi)

            Thus it came; give heed to 't.
My conscience first received a tenderness,
Scruple, and prick ... Thus hulling in
The wild sea of my conscience ... that's to say,
I meant to rectify my conscience, which
I then did feel full sick and yet not well...
            King Henry VIII (II, iv)

CONSCIENCE

There's nothing I have done yet, o' my conscience,
Deserves a corner . . . if my actions
Were tried by every tongue, every eye saw 'em. . .
I know my life so even.
    King Henry VIII (III, i)

So much my conscience whispers in your ear,
Which none but Heaven, and you, and I, shall hear.
    King John (I, i)

This is the excellent foppery of the world, that when we are sick in fortune—often the surfeit of our own behavior—we make guilty of our disasters the sun, the moon, and the stars, as if we were villains by necessity, fools by heavenly compulsion. . .
    King Lear (I, ii)

      . . . know'st thou not,
That, when the searching eye of heaven is hid
Behind the globe that lights the lower world,
Then thieves and robbers range abroad unseen,
In murders, and outrage bloody, here;
But when, from under this terrestrial ball,
He fires the proud tops of the eastern pines,
And darts his light through every guilty hole,
Then murders, treasons, and detested sins,
The cloak of night being pluck'd from off their backs,
Stand bare and naked, trembling at themselves? . . .
His treasons will sit blushing in his face,
Not able to endure the sight of day,
But, self-affrighted, tremble at his sin.
    King Richard II (III, ii)

Every man's conscience is a thousand swords. . .
    King Richard III (V, ii)

CONSCIENCE

Till sable Night, mother of Dread and Fear,
Upon the world dim darkness doth display,
And in her vaulty prison stows the Day...
  And every one to rest themselves betake,   [wake
  Save thieves and cares and troubled minds that
            Lucrece (stanzas 17-18)

O, what excuse can my invention make,
When thou shalt charge me with so black a deed?
Will not my tongue be mute, my frail joints shake,
Mine eyes forego their light, my false heart bleed?
The guilt being great, the fear doth still exceed;
  And extreme fear can neither fight nor fly,
  But coward-like with trembling terror die.
            Lucrece (stanza 33)

Think but how vile a spectacle it were,
To view thy present trespass in another.
Men's faults do seldom to themselves appear;
Their own transgressions partially they smother:
This guilt would seem death-worthy in thy brother.
  O, how are they wrapp'd in with infamies,
  That from their own misdeeds askance their eyes!
            Lucrece (stanza 91)

But they whose guilt within their bosoms lie
  Imagine every eye beholds their blame...
            Lucrece (stanza 192)

A dagger of the mind...
            Macbeth (II, i)

... full of scorpions is my mind...
            Macbeth (III, ii)

CONSCIENCE

Canst thou not minister to a mind diseased,
Pluck from the memory a rooted sorrow. . .
              Macbeth (V, iii)

              . . . it presses to my memory
Like damned guilty deeds to sinners' minds.
              Romeo and Juliet (III, ii)

For I am sham'd by that which I bring forth,
And so should you, to love things nothing worth.
              Sonnet LXXII

              O, it is monstrous! monstrous!
Methought the billows spoke, and told me of it;
The winds did sing it to me; and the thunder,
That deep and dreadful organ-pipe . . . did bass my
        trespass.
              The Tempest (III, iii)

              Their great guilt,
Like poison given to work a great time after,
Now 'gins to bite the spirits.
              The Tempest (III, iii)

I'll haunt thee like a wicked conscience still,
That mouldeth goblins swift as frenzy's thoughts.—
              Troilus and Cressida (V, xi)

CONSEQUENCE

All's well that ends well...
    All's Well That Ends Well (IV, iv)

What our contempt doth often hurl from us,
We wish it ours again...
    Antony and Cleopatra (I, ii)

Ten thousand harms, more than the ills I know,
My idleness doth hatch.
    Antony and Cleopatra (I, ii)

... for they say every why hath a wherefore.
    Comedy of Errors (II, ii)

    ... never shame to hear
What you have nobly done.
    Coriolanus (II, ii)

Sweets to the sweet...
    Hamlet (V, i)

      [wolf.
But since all is well, keep it so; wake not a sleeping
    King Henry IV, Part II (I, ii)

    The honor of it
Does pay the act of it, as, i' the contrary,
The foulness is the punishment.
    King Henry VIII (III, ii)

Nothing will come of nothing.
    King Lear (I, i)

    All friends shall taste
The wages of their virtue, and all foes
The cup of their deservings.
    King Lear (V, iii)

CONSEQUENCE

The wheel is come full circle...
        King Lear (V, iii)

Things sweet to taste prove in digestion sour.
        King Richard II (I, iii)

*   Naught's had, all's spent,*
Where our desire is got without content.
'Tis safer to be that which we destroy
Than by destruction dwell in doubtful joy.
        Macbeth (III, ii)

                                    [restraint?
Lucio: *Why, how now, Claudio! Whence comes this*
Claud: *From too much liberty, my Lucio, liberty.*
        ... every scope by the immoderate use
        Turns to restraint. Our natures do pursue,
        Like rats that ravin down their proper bane,
        A thirsty evil, and when we drink we die.
                Measure for Measure (I, ii)

Alack, when once our grace we have forgot,
Nothing goes right.
        Measure for Measure (IV, iv)

Hast still pays hast, and leisure answers leisure,
Like doth quit like, and measure still for measure.
        Measure for Measure (V, i)

The error or our eye directs our mind;
What error leads, must err.
        Troilus and Cressida (V, ii)

Thus have I shunned the fire for fear of burning,
And drench'd me in the sea, where I am drown'd.
        Two Gentlemen of Verona (I, iii)

CONTENTION

Would we were all of one mind, and one mind good.
Cymbeline (V, iv)

Beware of entrance to a quarrel; but being in,
Bear't that the opposed may beware of thee.
Hamlet (I, iii)

Civil dissension is a viperous worm...
This late dissension, grown betwixt the peers,
Burns under feigned ashes of forg'd love,
And will at last break out into a flame...
King Henry VI, Part I (III, i)

But more, when envy breeds unkind division;
There comes the ruin, there begins confusion.
King Henry VI, Part I (IV, i)

Good Lord! what madness rules in brain-sick men,
When, for so slight and frivolous a cause,
Such factious emulations shall arise! ...
Confounded be your strife!
And perish ye, with your audacious prate!
Presumptuous vassals! are you not asham'd
With this immodest clamorous outrage...
King Henry VI, Part I (IV, i)

I see thy fury: if I longer stay,
We shall begin our ancient bickerings.—
King Henry VI, Part II (I, i)

For blessed are the peacemakers on earth...
How irksome is this music to my heart!
When such strings jar, what hope of harmony?
I pray, my Lords, let me compound this strife.
King Henry VI, Part II (II, i)

CONTENTION

The times are wild; contention, like a horse
Full of high feeding, madly hath broke loose
And bears down all before him.
            King Henry IV, Part II (I, i)

If we do now make our atonement well,
Our peace will, like a broken limb united.
Grow stronger for the breaking.
            King Henry IV, Part II (IV, i)

Turning the word to sword, and life to death.
            King Henry IV, Part II (IV, ii)

Nay, then, this spark will prove a raging fire,
If wind and fuel be brought to feed it with. . .
            King Henry VI, Part II (III, i)

A little gale will soon disperse that cloud. . .
For every cloud engenders not a storm.
            King Henry VI, Part III (V, iii)

To be a make-peace shall become my age: —
            King Richard II (I, i)

If he do fear God, he must necessarily keep peace; if
he break the peace, he ought to enter into a quarrel
with fear and trembling.
            Much Ado About Nothing (II, iii)

In a false quarrel there is no true valour.
            Much Ado About Nothing (V, i)

                    O, virtuous fight,
When right with right wars who shall be most right!
            Troilus and Cressida (III, ii)

COUNTENANCE

The tartness of his face sours ripe grapes.
                Coriolanus (V, iv)

I have heard of your paintings too, well enough;
God hath given you one face, and you make
        yourselves another...
               Hamlet (III, i)

                  ...get thee gone for I do see,
Danger and disobedience in thine eye.
                King Henry IV, Part I (I, iii)

Why, I can smile, and murder whiles I smile...
And wet my cheeks with artificial tears,
And frame my face to all occasions...
Deceive more slily than Ulysses could...
                King Henry VI, Part III (III, ii)

                    ... securely I espy
Virtue with valour couched in thine eye.
                King Richard II (I, iii)

Beauty is bought by judgment of the eye.
                Love's Labour's Lost (II, i)

Then my digression is so vile, so base,
That it will live engraven in my face.
                Lucrece (stanza 29)

                    There's no art
To find the mind's construction in the face.
                Macbeth (I, iv)

COUNTENANCE

Nature hath framed strange fellows in her time—
Some that will evermore peep through their eyes,
And laugh like parrots at a bagpiper,
And other of such vinegar aspect
That they'll not show their teeth in way of smile...
          Merchant of Venice (I, i)

Oh, she doth teach the torches to burn bright!
It seems she hangs upon the cheek of night
Like a rich jewel in an Ethiop's ear—
Beauty too rich for use, for earth too dear!
          Romeo and Juliet (I, v)

... thou shamest the music of sweet news
By playing it to me with so sour a face.
          Romeo and Juliet (II, v)

Shall I compare thee to a summer's day?
Thou art more lovely and more temperate...
          Sonnet XVIII

... 'tis the mind that makes the body rich,
... as the sun breaks through the darkest clouds,
So honor peereth in the meanest habit.
... is the jay more precious than the lark
Because his feathers are more beautiful?
          Taming of the Shrew (IV, iii)

...the heart that dies in tempest of thy angry frown.
          Titus Andronicus (I, i)

... thy smiles become thee well...
          Twelfth Night (II, v)

For looks kill love, and love by looks reviveth...
          Venus and Adonis (stanza 78)

COURAGE

Boldness be my friend!
Arm me, audacity, from head to foot!
  Cymbeline (I, vi)

. . . nothing routs us but
The villainy of our fears.
  Cymbeline (V, ii)

                    These three,
Three thousand confident, in act as many,—
For three performers are the file, when all
The rest do nothing,—with this word, <u>*stand!*</u> <u>*stand!*</u>
  Cymbeline (V, iii)

Cowards die many times before their deaths,
The valiant never taste of death but once.
Of all the wonders that I yet have heard,
It seems to me most strange that men should fear,
Seeing that death, a necessary end,
Will come when it will come.
  Julius Caesar (II, ii)

. . . hollow men. . .
Make gallant show and promise of their mettle,
But when they should endure the bloody spur,
They fall their crests and like deceitful jades
Sink in the trial.
  Julius Caesar (IV, ii)

Of all base passions, fear is most accursed. . .
  King Henry VI (V, ii)

COURAGE

My lord, wise men ne'er sit and wail their woes,
But presently prevent the ways to wail.
To fear the foe, since fear oppresseth strength,
Gives, in your weakness, strength unto your foe.
And so your follies fight against yourself.
  King Richard II (III, ii)

          Present fears
Are less than horrible imaginings.
  Macbeth (I, iii)

            When our actions do not,
Our fears do make us traitors.
  Macbeth (IV, ii)

            Our doubts are traitors,
And make us lose the good we oft might win
By fearing to attempt.
  Measure for Measure (I, iv)

I know not by what power I am made bold. . .
  Midsummer Night's Dream (I, i)

              . . . bootless speed
When cowardice pursues, and valor flies.
  Midsummer Night's Dream (II, i)

DEATH

Now, my spirit is going. . .
    Antony and Cleopatra (IV, xv)

The ground that gave them first has them again:
Their pleasures here are past, so is their pain.
    Cymbeline (IV, ii)

      . . . he had rather
Groan so in perpetuity, than be cur'd
By the sure physician, death, who is the key
To unbar these locks.
    Cymbeline (V, iv)

By med'cine life may be prolong'd, yet death
Will seize the doctor too.
    Cymbeline (V, v)

      —To die, to sleep,—
No more; and by a sleep to say we end
The heart-ache, and the thousand natural shocks
That flesh is heir to?—'tis a consummation
Devoutly to be wish'd. To die, to sleep;—
To sleep, perchance, to dream;—ay, there's the rub;
For in that sleep of death what dreams may come,
When we have shuffled off this mortal coil,
Must give us pause . . . the dread of something after
   death,—
The undiscover'd country, from whose bourn
No traveller returns,—puzzles the will,
And makes us rather bear those ills we have,
Than fly to others that we know not of.
    Hamlet (III, i)

And flights of angels sing thee to thy rest!—
    Hamlet (V, ii)

DEATH

Time is come round,
And where I did begin, there shall I end,
My life is run his compass.
Julius Caesar (V, iii)

When that this body did contain a spirit...
King Henry IV, Part I (V, iv)

When Heaven shall call her from this cloud of darkness...
King Henry VIII (V, v)

Men must endure
Their going hence, even as their coming hither.
Ripeness (readiness) is all.
King Lear (V, ii)

By this time...
One of our souls had wandered in the air,
Banish'd this frail sepulchre of our flesh...
King Richard II (I, iii)

Since presently your souls must part your bodies.
King Richard II (III, i)

... it is a knell
That summons thee to Heaven or to Hell.
Macbeth (II, i)

Aye, but to die, and go we know not where...
The weariest and most loathed worldly life
That age, ache, penury, and imprisonment
Can lay on nature is a paradise
To what we fear of death.
Measure for Measure (III, i)

DEATH

That life is better life, past fearing death,
Than that which lives to fear.
                    Measure for Measure (V, i)

But that a joy past joy calls out on me,
It were a grief so brief to part with thee.
                    Romeo and Juliet (III, iii)

Death lies on her like an untimely frost
Upon the sweetest flower of all the field.
                    Romeo and Juliet (IV, v)

                    Heaven and yourself
Had part in this fair maid, now Heaven hath all.
And all the better is it for the maid.
Your part in her you could not keep from death,
But Heaven keeps his part in eternal life...
And weep ye now, seeing she is advanced
Above the clouds, as high as Heaven itself?
                    Romeo and Juliet (IV, v)

For though fond nature bids us all lament,
Yet nature's tears are reason's merriment.
                    Romeo and Juliet (IV, v)

... shake the yoke of inauspicious stars
From this world-wearied flesh.
                    Romeo and Juliet (V, iii)

And call him to long peace.
                    Timon of Athens (I, ii)

DEBT

Yet fortune cannot recompense me better,
Than to die well, and not my master's debtor.
   As You Like It (II, iii)

Neither a borrower nor a lender be;
For loan oft loses both itself and friend,
And borrowing dulls the edge of husbandry.
   Hamlet (I, iii)

I can get no remedy against this consumption of the purse. Borrowing only lingers and lingers it out, but the disease is incurable.
   King Henry IV, Part II (I, ii)

A fool's bolt is soon shot.
   King Henry V (III, vii)

That which I owe is lost.
   Merchant of Venice (I, i)

He that dies pays all debts.
   The Tempest (III, ii)

They have e'en put my breath from me, the slaves. Creditors? Devils!
   Timon of Athens (III, iv)

DEITY

. . . and He that doth the ravens feed,
Yea, providently caters for the sparrow,
Be comfort to my age!
As You Like It (II, iii)

Why, even in that was heaven ordinant. . .
Hamlet (V, ii)

He is a great observer, and he looks
Quite through the deeds of men.
Julius Caesar (I, ii)

O, thou eternal mover of the heavens. . .
King Henry VI, Part II (III, iii)

Heaven is above all yet, There sits a judge
That no king can corrupt.
King Henry VIII (III, i)

And even there, methinks, an angel spake. . .
To give us warrant from the hand of heaven. . .
King John (V, ii)

Now, He that made me, knows. . .
King Richard II (II, i)

God's a good man . . . but, God is to be worshipped.
Much Ado About Nothing (III, v)

. . . He that hath the steerage of my course
Direct my sail!
Romeo and Juliet (I, iv)

DEPRESSION

Sweet recreation barred, what doth ensue
But moody and dull Melancholy...
            Comedy of Errors (V, i)

            We are not ourselves
When nature being oppressed commands the mind
To suffer with the body.
         King Lear (II, iv)

So should my thoughts be severed from my griefs,
And woes by wrong imaginations lose
The knowledge of themselves.
         King Lear (IV, vi)

            ... I am bound
Upon a wheel of fire that mine own tears
Do scald like molten lead.
         King Lear (IV, vii)

Antonio: In sooth, I know not why I am so sad.
         It wearies me, you say it wearies you;
         But how I caught it, found it, or came by it,
         What stuff 'tis made of, whereof it is born,
         I am to learn.
         And such a want-wit sadness makes of me
         That I have much ado to know myself.
Salario: Your mind is tossing on the ocean—
         Merchant of Venice (I, i)

You have too much respect upon the world.
They lose it that do buy it with much care.
         Merchant of Venice (I, i)

And melancholy is the nurse of frenzy.
         Taming of the Shrew (induction)

DEVIL

He's a disease that must be cut away.
                Coriolanus (III, i)

These lies are like the father that begets them; gross as a mountain, open, palpable.
                King Henry IV, Part I (II, iv)

Give the devil his due.
                King Henry V (III, vii)

. . . that same purpose-changer, that sly devil,
That broker, that still breaks the pate of faith;
That daily break-vow; he that wins of all,
Of kings, of beggars, old men, young men, maids,—
Who having no external thing to lose
But the word maid, cheats the poor maid of that;
That smooth-fac'd gentleman. . .
                King John (II, ii)

Thou'rt damn'd as black—nay, nothing is so black;
Thou art more deep damn'd than prince Lucifer. . .
                King John (IV, iii)

What, do you tremble? are you all afraid?
Alas, I blame you not, for you are mortal,
And mortal eyes cannot endure the devil.—
Avaunt, thou dreadful minister of hell!
                King Richard III (I, ii)

What, can the Devil speak true?
                Macbeth (I, iii)

. . . the devil: consider, he's an enemy to mankind.
                Twelfth Night (III, iv)

EARTHLY PROBATION

The web of our life is of a mingled yarn, good and ill together: our virtues would be proud, if our faults whipped them not, and our crimes would despair, if they were not cherished by our virtues.
  All's Well That Ends Well (IV, iii)

*A rarer spirit never
Did steer Humanity; but you, gods, will give us
Some faults to make us men.*
  Antony and Cleopatra (V, i)

*Thou seest we are not all along unhappy:
This wide and universal theatre
Presents more woeful pageants than the scene
Wherein we play in. All the world's a stage
And all the men and women merely players...*
  As You Like It (II, vii)

... how brief the life of man...
  As You Like It (III, ii)

... here we wander in illusions.
  Comedy of Errors (IV, iii)

What a piece of work is a man! how noble in reason! how infinite in faculty! in form and moving how express and admirable! in action how like an angel! in apprehension how like a god! the beauty of the world!
  Hamlet (II, ii)

*Sure, he that made us with such large discourse,
Looking before and after, gave us not
That capability and god-like reason
To fust in us unus'd.*
  Hamlet (IV, iv)

EARTHLY PROBATION

Lord, we know what we are, but know not what we may be. God be at your table!
  Hamlet (IV, v)

There's a divinity that shapes our ends,
Rough-hew them how we will...
(In Stratford on Avon, hedge-cutters use this same terminology even today. One hedge-cutter 'rough hews' the hedge and the second hedge-cutter 'shapes the ends' or, in other words, does the fine trimming.)
  Hamlet (V, ii)

O, let the vile world end,
And the premised flames of the last day
Knit heaven and earth together!
Now let the general trumpet blow his blast...
  King Henry VI, Part II (V, ii)

Lo, now my glory smear'd in dust and blood!
My parks, my walks, my manors that I had,
Even now forsake me; and of all my lands,
Is nothing left me, but my body's length!
Why, what is pomp, rule, reign, but earth and dust?
And, live we how we can, yet die we must.
  King Henry VI, Part III (V, ii)

When we are born, we cry that we are come
To this great stage of fools.
  King Lear (IV, vi)

... for what I speak
My body shall make good upon this earth,
Or my divine soul answer it in heaven.
  King Richard II (I, i)

EARTHLY PROBATION

All places that the eye of heaven visits,
Are to a wise man ports and happy havens...
            King Richard II (I, iii)

The pale-fac'd moon looks bloody on the earth,
And lean-look'd prophets whisper fearful change...
            King Richard II (II, iv)

I live with bread like you, feel want, taste grief,
Need friends...
                King Richard II (III, ii)

... upon this bank and shoal of time...
            Macbeth (I, vii)

                    ... every one
According to the gift which bounteous Nature
Hath in him closed, whereby he does receive
Particular addition from the bill
That writes them all alike.
            Macbeth (III, i)

And you all know security
Is mortals' chiefest enemy.
            Macbeth (III, v)

I am in this earthly world, where to do harm
Is often laudable, to do good sometime
Accounted dangerous folly.
            Macbeth (IV, ii)

... that which should accompany old age,
... honour, love, obedience, troops of friends...
            Macbeth (V, iii)

EARTHLY PROBATION

Tomorrow, and tomorrow, and tomorrow
Creeps in this petty pace from day to day,
To the last syllable of recorded time,
And all our yesterdays have lighted fools
The way to dusty death. Out, out, brief candle!
Life's but a walking shadow, a poor player
That struts and frets his hour upon the stage
And then is heard no more. It is a tale
Told by an idiot, full of sound and fury,
Signifying nothing.
     Macbeth (V, v)

Lord, what fools these mortals be!
    Midsummer Night's Dream (III, ii)

Antiochus, I thank thee, who hath taught
My frail mortality to know itself. . .
For death remember'd should be like a mirror,
Who tells us life's but breath, to trust it error.
    Pericles (I, i)

    . . . I talk of dreams
Which are the children of an idle brain,
Begot of nothing but vain fantasy,
Which is as thin of substance as the air
And more inconstant than the wind. . .
    Romeo and Juliet (I, iv)

Such wind as scatters young men through the world
To seek their fortunes farther than at home,
Where small experience grows.
    Taming of the Shrew (I, ii)

EARTHLY PROBATION

> *. . . Hell is empty,*
> *And all the devils are here.*
> *The Tempest (I, ii)*

> *And, like the baseless fabric of this vision,*
> *The cloud-capp'd towers, the gorgeous palaces,*
> *The solemn temples, the great globe itself,*
> *Yea, all which it inherit, shall dissolve,*
> *And, like this insubstantial pageant faded,*
> *Leave not a rack behind. We are such stuff*
> *As dreams are made on, and our little life*
> *Is rounded with a sleep.*
> *The Tempest (IV, i)*

> *O, wonder!*
> *How many goodly creatures are there here!*
> *How beauteous mankind is! O brave new world,*
> *That has such people in't!*
> *The Tempest (V, i)*

> *. . . life's uncertain voyage. . .*
> *Timon of Athens (V, i)*

> *A spirit I am indeed:*
> *But am in that dimension grossly clad,*
> *Which from the womb I did participate.*
> *Twelfth Night (V, i)*

FAITH

There are no tricks in plain and simple faith.
                Julius Caesar (IV, ii)

Oh, that a man might know
The end of this day's business ere it come!
But it sufficeth that the day will end,
And then the end is known.
                Julius Caesar (V, i)

Gloucester: I hope they will not come upon us now.
King Henry: We are in God's hand, brother, not in
            theirs.
                King Henry V (III, vi)

Now, God be prais'd! that to believing souls
Gives light in darkness, comfort in despair!
                King Henry VI, Part II (II, i)

But heaven hath a hand in these events. . .
                King Richard II (V, ii)

O momentary grace of mortal men,
Which we more hunt for than the grace of God!
Who builds his hope in air of your fair looks,
Lives like a drunken sailor on a mast,
Ready with every nod to tumble down
Into the fatal bowels of the deep.
                King Richard III (III, iv)

The mind I sway by and the heart I bear
Shall never sag with doubt nor shake with fear.
                Macbeth (V, ii)

. . . to be saved by believing rightly. . .
                Twelfth Night (III, ii)

FAMILY

Youth, thou bear'st thy father's face...
    All's Well That Ends Well (I, ii)

    O disloyal thing
That shouldst repair my youth, thou heap'st
A year's age on me!
    Cymbeline (I, i)

    You sin against
Obedience, which you owe your father.
    Cymbeline (II, iii)

And with no less nobility of love
Than that which dearest father bears his son...
    Hamlet (I, ii)

O, Jephthah, judge of Israel,—what a treasure hadst
thou! . . . One fair daughter...
    Hamlet (II, ii)

How chance, thou art not with the prince thy brother?
He loves thee, and thou dost neglect him, Thomas.
Thou hast a better place in his affection
Than all thy brothers; cherish it, my boy...
Omit him not; blunt not his love
Nor lose the good advantage of his grace
By seeming cold, or careless of his will...
Chide him for faults, and do it reverently,
When you perceive his blood inclin'd to mirth.
But, being moody, give him line and scope,
Till that his passions, like a whale on ground,
Confound themselves with working. Learn this...
And thou shalt prove a shelter to thy friends;
A hoop of gold, to bind thy brothers in...
    King Henry IV, Part II (IV, iv)

FAMILY

I'll be your father and your brother too;
Let me but bear your love, I'll bear your cares.
              King Henry IV, Part II (V, ii)

Look back into your mighty ancestors...
The blood and courage, that renowned them,
Runs in your veins...
              King Henry V (I, ii)

Hath love in thy old blood no living fire?
Edward's seven sons, whereof thyself art one,
Were as seven phials of his sacred blood,
Or seven fair branches springing from one root...
              King Richard II (I, ii)

O thou, the earthly author of my blood,—
Whose youthful spirit in me regenerate...
              King Richard II (I, iii)

O, had thy grandsire, with a prophet's eye,
Seen how his son's son should destroy his sons...
              King Richard II (II, i)

A grandam's name is little less in love
Than is the doting title of a mother;
They are as children but one step below,
Even of your mettle, of your very blood;
Of all one pain, save for a night of groans
Endur'd of her, for whom you bid like sorrow.
              King Richard III (IV, iv)

              ... I often did behold
In thy sweet semblance my old age new born...
              Lucrece (stanza 252)

FAMILY

> *. . . it was my own, part of my heritage,*
> *Which my dead father did bequeath to me. . .*
> *It kept where I kept, I so dearly lov'd it;*
> *Pericles (I, i)*

From fairest creatures we desire increase,
That thereby beauty's rose might never die. . .
Sonnet I

Look in thy glass, and tell the face thou viewest,
Now is the time that face should form another. . .
Or who is he so fond will be the tomb
Of his self-love, to stop posterity?
Thou art thy mother's glass, and she in thee
Calls back the lovely April of her prime. . .
> *Die single, and thine image dies with thee.*
> *Sonnet III*

That's for thyself to breed another thee,
Or ten times happier, be it ten for one;
Ten times thyself were happier than thou art,
If ten of thine ten times refigur'd thee:
Then what could death do if thou shouldst depart,
Leaving thee living in posterity?
> *Be not self-will'd for thou art much too fair*
> *To be Death's conquest; make worms thine heir.*
> *Sonnet VI*

Resembling sire and child and happy mother,
Who, all in one, one pleasing note do sing:
Whose speechless song, being many, seeming one. . .
> *Sonnet VIII*

When every private widow well may keep,
By children's eyes, her husband's shape in mind.
> *Sonnet IX*

FAMILY

Whom [Nature] best endow'd, she gave thee more;
Which bounteous gift thou shouldst in bounty cherish;
She carv'd thee for her seal, and meant thereby
Thou shouldst print more, nor let that copy die.
Sonnet XI

Now all the blessings
Of a glad father compass thee about!
The Tempest (V, i)

Then let my father's honours live in me...
Titus Andronicus (I, i)

... Thy grandsire lov'd thee well:
Many a time he danc'd thee on his knee,
Sung thee asleep, his loving breast thy pillow...
Titus Andronicus (V, iii)

'Tis beauty truly blent, whose red and white
Nature's own sweet and cunning hand laid on:
Lady, you are the cruel'st she alive,
If you will lead these graces to the grave,
And leave the world no copy.
Twelfth Night (I, v)

Upon the earth's increase why shouldst thou feed,
Unless the earth with thy increase be fed?
By law of nature thou art bound to breed,
That thine may live, when thou thyself art dead;
And do, in spite of death, thou dost survive,
In that thy likeness still is left alive.
Venus and Adonis (stanza 29)

FLATTERY

. . . that which melteth fools—I mean sweet words,
Low-crooked curtsies, and base spaniel fawning.
  Julius Caesar (III, i)

...you...think with wagging of your tongue to win me...
  King Henry VIII (V, iii)

He cannot flatter, he—
An honest mind and plain—he must speak truth!
  King Lear (II, ii)

He that loves to be flattered is worthy o' the flatterer.
  Timon of Athens (I, i)

Oh, that men's ears should be
To counsel deaf, but not to flattery!
  Timon of Athens (I, ii)

Ah, when the means are gone that buy this praise,
The breath is gone whereof this praise is made.
  Timon of Athens (II, ii)

FORGIVENESS

If it might please you, to enforce no further
The griefs between ye. To forget them quite
Were to remember that the present need
Speaks to atone you.
                    Antony and Cleopatra (II, ii)

Think'st thou it honorable for a noble man
Still to remember wrongs?
                Coriolanus (V, iii)

                    Kneel not to me;
The power that I have on you is to spare you;
The malice towards you to forgive you. Live,
And deal with others better.
                Cymbeline (V, v)

Exchange forgiveness with me...
                Hamlet (V, ii)

Forgive the comment that my passion made...
                King John (IV, ii)

Wrath-kindled gentlemen...
Let's purge this choler without letting blood;
This we prescribe, though no physician;
Deep malice makes too deep incision:
Forget, forgive; conclude, and be agreed...
                King Richard II (I, i)

Duchess: *Say—pardon, king; let pity teach thee how.*
           The word is short, but not so short as sweet.
King: *I pardon him, as God shall pardon me.*
              King Richard II (V, iii)

FORGIVENESS

Though with their high wrongs I am struck to the [quick,
Yet, with my nobler reason 'gainst my fury
Do I take part. The rarer action is
In virtue than in vengeance: they being penitent,
The sole drift of my purpose doth extend
Not a frown further.
                    The Tempest (V, i)

And my ending is despair,
Unless I be reliev'd by prayer,
Which pierces so, that it assaults
Mercy itself, and frees all faults.
As you from crimes would pardon'd be,
Let your indulgence set me free.
                    The Tempest (V, i)

And at my suit, sweet, pardon what is past.
                    Titus Andronicus (I, i)

To revenge is no valor, but to bear.
                    Timon of Athens (III, v)

FRIENDSHIP

Love all, trust a few,
Do wrong to none; be able for thine enemy
Rather in power, than use; and keep thy friend
Under thy own life's key. . .
All's Well That Ends Well (I, i)

Nature teaches beasts to know their friends.
Coriolanus (II, i)

Be thou familiar, but by no means vulgar.
The friends thou hast, and their adoption tried,
Grapple them to thy soul with hoops of steel. . .
Hamlet (I, iii)

"Et tu, Brute?". . .
This was the most unkindest cut of all. . .
Julius Caesar (III, i & ii)

Thou hast described
A hot friend cooling. Ever note. . .
When love begins to sicken and decay,
It useth an enforced ceremony.
Julius Caesar (IV, ii)

A friend should bear his friend's infirmities. . .
Julius Caesar (IV, iii)

My heart doth joy that yet in all my life
I found no man but he was true to me.
Julius Caesar (V, v)

. . . I see virtue in his looks. If then the tree may be known by the fruit, as the fruit by the tree, then, peremptorily I speak it, there is virtue in that Falstaff; him keep with, the rest banish.
King Henry IV, Part I (II, iv)

FRIENDSHIP

There is flattery in friendship.
King Henry V (III, vii)

And I have heard it said, unbidden guests
Are often welcomest when they are gone.
King Henry VI, Part I (II, ii)

. . . those you make friends
And give your hearts to, when they once perceive
The least rub in your fortunes, fall away
Like water from ye. . .
King Henry VIII (II, i)

Who alone suffers suffers most i' the mind,
Leaving free things and happy shows behind.
But then the mind much sufferance doth o'erskip
When grief hath mates, and bearing fellowship.
King Lear (III, vi)

If music and sweet poetry agree,
As they must needs, the sister and the brother,
Then must the love be great 'twixt thee and me,
Because thou lov'st the one, and I the other.
Passionate Pilgrim (VI)

Faithful friends are hard to find. . .
He that is thy friend indeed,
He will help thee in thy need;
If thou sorrow, he will weep;
If thou wake, he cannot sleep:
Thus of every grief in heart
He with thee doth bear a part.
These are certain signs to know
Faithful friend from flattering foe.
Passionate Pilgrim (XX)

FRIENDSHIP

Then you love us, we you, and we'll clasp hands;
When peers thus knit, a kingdom ever stands.
              Pericles (II, iv)

    . . . 'twixt such friends as we
Few words suffice.
              Taming of the Shrew (I, ii)

    . . . ceremony was but devised at first
To set a gloss on faint deeds, hollow welcomes. . .
But where there is true friendship, there needs none.
              Timon of Athens (I, ii)

. . . what need we have any friends if we should ne'er have need of 'em? They were the most needless creatures living should we ne'er have use for 'em, and would most resemble sweet instruments hung up in cases that keep their sound to themselves.
              Timon of Athens (I, ii)

. . . when no friends are by, men praise themselves.
              Titus andronicus (V, iii)

They that thrive well take counsel of their friends.
              Venus and Adonis (stanza 107)

GOSSIP

The nature of bad news infects the teller.
Antony and Cleopatra (I, ii)

For slander lives upon succession,
Forever housed where it gets possession.
Comedy of Errors (III, i)

Ill deeds are doubled with an evil word.
Comedy of Errors (III, ii)

It is an office of the gods to venge it,
Not mine to speak on't.
Cymbeline (I, vi)

'Tis slander,
Whose edge is sharper than the sword; whose tongue
Outvenoms all the worms of Nile; whose breath
Rides on the posting winds, and doth belie
All corners of the world...
Cymbeline (III, iv)

... the people muddied,
Thick and unwholesome in their thoughts and whispers...
Hamlet (IV, v)

Upon my tongue continual slanders ride,
The which in every language I pronounce,
Stuffing the ears of men with false reports.
I speak of peace, while covert enmity,
Under the smile of safety, wounds the world...
And not a man of them brings other news [tongues
Than they have learn'd of me. From Rumour's
They bring smooth comforts false, worse than true wrongs.
King Henry IV, Part II (induction)

GOSSIP

Rumour doth double, like the voice and echo...
King Henry IV, Part II (III, i)

I am richer than my base accusers,
That never knew what truth meant.
King Henry VIII (II, i)

Sal: What other harm have I good lady, done,
But spoke the harm that is by others done?
Con: Which harm within itself so heinous is,
As it makes harmful all that speak of it.
King John (III, i)

Fool: Thou canst tell why one's nose stands i' the middle on's face?
Lear: No.
Fool: Why, to keep one's eyes of either side 's nose, that what a man cannot smell out he may spy into.
King Lear (I, v)

Report is changeable.
King Lear (VI, vii)

I am disgrac'd, impeach'd, and baffled here;
Pierc'd to the soul with slander's venom'd spear;
The which no balm can cure...
King Richard II (I, i)

Luc: ... I can tell thee pretty tales...
Vin: You have told me too many of him already, sire if they be true. If not true, none were enough.
Measure for Measure (IV, iii)

GOSSIP

Done to death by slanderous tongues
Was the Hero that here lies...
                Much Ado About Nothing (V, iii)

Who steals my purse steals trash...
But he that filches from me my good name,
Robs me of that which not enriches him,
And makes me poor indeed.
                Othello (III, iii)

Two may keep counsel, putting one away.
                Romeo and Juliet (II, iv)

That thou art blam'd shall not be thy defect,
For slander's mark was ever yet the fair;
The ornament of beauty is suspect,
A crow that flies in heaven's sweetest air.
So thou be good, slander doth but approve
Thy worth the greater, being woo'd of time;
For canker vice the sweetest buds doth love,
And thou present'st a pure unstained prime.
                Sonnet LXX

A slave whose gall coins slanders like a mint...
                Troilus and Cressida (I, iii)

GRATITUDE

Inspired merit so by breath is barr'd:
It is not so with him that all things knows,
As 't is with us that square our guess by shows:
But most it is presumption in us, when
The help of heaven we count the act of men.
                All's Well That Ends Well (II, i)

Blow, blow, thou winter wind,
Thou art not so unkind
As man's ingratitude. . .
             As You Like It (II, vii)

Ingratitude is monstrous.
             Coriolanus (II, iii)

        Sir, we have all
Great cause to give great thanks.
             Coriolanus (V, iv)

I have been debtor to you for courtesies, which I will
be ever to pay, and yet pay still.
             Cymbeline (I, iv)

Your very goodness, and your company,
O'erpays all I can do.
             Cymbeline (II, iv)

            Beggar that I am,
I am even poor in thanks; but I thank you. . .
             Hamlet (II, ii)

Ingratitude, thou marble-hearted fiend,
More hideous when thou show'st thee in a child
Than the sea monster!
             King Lear (I, iv)

GRATITUDE

The means that heaven yields must be embrac'd,
And not neglected; else, if heaven would,
And we will not, heaven's offer we refuse,
The proffer'd means of succour and redress.
    King Richard II (III, ii)

      God is much displeas'd,
That you take with unthankfulness his doing:
In common worldly things, 'tis call'd ungrateful,
With dull unwillingness to repay a debt,
Which with a bounteous hand was kindly lent...
    King Richard III (II, ii)

      Happy thou art not,
For what thou hast not, still thou strivest to get,
And what thou hast, forget'st
    Measure for Measure (III, i)

... there's my purse; I am yet thy debtor.
    Merry Wives of Windsor (II, ii)

... what we have we prize not to the worth,
Whiles we enjoy it; but being lack'd and lost,
Why, then we rack the value; then we find
The virtue, that possession would not show us
Whiles it was ours.
    Much Ado About Nothing (IV, i)

... if that ever my low fortune's better,
I'll pay your bounties; till then rest your debtor.
    Pericles (II, i)

My recompense is thanks, that's all;
Yet my good will is great, though the gift small.
    Pericles (III, iv)

GRATITUDE

A pack of blessings lights upon thy back;
Happiness courts thee in her best array;
But, like a misbehav'd and sullen wench,
Thou pout'st upon thy fortune and thy love.
Take heed, take heed, for such die miserable.
                Romeo and Juliet (III, iii)

He receives comfort like cold porridge.
                The Tempest (II, i)

I hate ingratitude more in a man,
Than lying, vainness, babbling, drunkenness,
Or any taint or vice, whose strong corruption
Inhabits our frail blood.
                Twelfth Night (III, v)

Injurious wasps! to feed on such sweet honey,
And kill the bees, that yield it, with your stings!
                Two Gentlemen of Verona (I, ii)

*   . . . time as long again*
Would be fill'd up, my brother, with our thanks;
And yet we should, for perpetuity,
Go hence in debt: and therefore, like a cipher,
Yet standing in rich place, I multiply,
With one we-thank-you, many thousands more
That go before it.
                Winter's Tale (I, ii)

GREED

Where none will sweat but for promotion;
And having that, do choke their service up
Even with the having. . .
>*As You Like It (II, iii)*

How many fond fools serve mad jealousy!
>*Comedy of Errors (II, i)*

All gold and silver rather turn to dirt!
As 'tis no better reckon'd,
But of those who worship dirty gods.
>*Cymbeline (III, vi)*

How quickly nature falls into revolt,
When gold becomes her object!
>*King Henry IV, Part II (IV, iv)*

>*. . . fling away ambition.*
By that sin fell the angels. How can man, then,
The image of his Maker, hope to win by it?
>*King Henry VIII (III, ii)*

Well, whiles I am a beggar, I will rail
And say,—there is no sin but to be rich;
And being rich, my virtue then shall be,
To say,—there is no vice but beggary. . .
Gain, be my lord! for I will worship thee!
>*King John (II, ii)*

Striving to better, oft we mar what's well.
>*King Lear (I, iv)*

Which, having all, all could not satisfy;
But poorly rich, so wanteth in his store,
That, cloy'd with much, he pineth still for more.
>*Lucrece (stanza 14)*

GREED

As one of which Tarquin lie revolving
The sundry danger of his will's obtaining;
Yet ever to obtain his will resolving,
Though weak-built hopes persuade him to abstaining;
Despair to gain doth traffic oft for gaining;
   And when great treasure is the meed propos'd
   Tho' death be adjunct, there's no death suppos'd.

Those that much covet are with gain so fond,
For what they have not, that which they possess,
They scatter and unloose it from their bond,
And so, by hoping more, they have but less;
Or, gaining more, the profit of excess
   Is but to surfeit, and such griefs sustain,
   That they prove bankrupt in this poor-rich gain.

The aim of all is but to nurse the life
With honour, wealth, and ease, in waning age;
And in this aim there is such thwarting strife,
That one for all, or all for one we gage:
As life for honour in fell battles' rage,
   Honour for wealth; and oft that wealth doth cost
   The death of all, and all together lost.

So that in venturing ill we leave to be
The things we are for that which we expect;
And this ambitious-foul infirmity,
In having much, torments us with defect
Of that we have: so then we do neglect
   The thing we have, and, all for want of wit,
   Make something nothing by augmenting it.
                Lucrece (stanzas 19-22)

...They say, if money go before, all ways do lie open.
            Merry Wives of Windsor (II, ii)

GREED

*O, what a world of vile ill-favour'd faults
Looks handsome in three hundred pounds a year!*
   Merry Wives of Windsor (III, iv)

*. . . a surfeit of the sweetest things
The deepest loathing to the stomach brings.*
   Midsummer Night's Dream (II, ii)

*The sweet honey
Is loathsome in his own deliciousness. . .*
   Romeo and Juliet (II, vi)

*The world is not thy friend, nor the world's law.
The world affords no law to make thee rich. . .*
   Romeo and Juliet (V, i)

*There is thy gold, worse poison to men's souls,
Doing more murder in this loathsome world
Than [this] . . . poison, thou hast sold me. . .*
   Romeo and Juliet (V, i)

*Then every thing includes itself in power,
Power into will, will into appetite;
And appetite, an universal wolf,
So doubly seconded with will and power,
Must make perforce an universal prey,
And, last, eat up himself.*
   Troilus and Cressida (I, iii)

*. . . place, riches and favour,
Prizes of accident as oft as merit:
Which when they fall, as being slippery standers,
The love that lean'd on them as slippery too,
Do one pluck down another, and together
Die in the fall.*
   Troilus and Cressida (III, iii)

HEALTH

Though I look old, yet I am strong...
For in my youth I never did apply
Hot and rebellious liquors in my blood...
                As You Like It (II, iii)

The crickets sing, and man's o'er-labour'd sense
Repairs itself by rest.
                Cymbeline (II, ii)

There's no room for faith, truth, nor honesty, in this
bosom of thine; 'tis all filled up with guts and midriff.
                King Henry IV, Part I (III, iii)

—O sleep! O gentle sleep! Nature's soft nurse...
                King Henry IV, Part II (III, i)

... with wine and wassail so convince
That memory, the warder of the brain,
Shall be a fume...
                Macbeth (I, vii)

                        ... the innocent sleep,
Sleep that knits up the raveled sleave of care,
The death of each day's life, sore labor's bath,
Balm of hurt minds, great nature's second course,
Chief nourisher in life's feast—
                Macbeth (II, ii)

Shake off this downy sleep, death's counterfeit...
                Macbeth (II, iii)

And drink, sir, is a great provoker...
                Macbeth (II, iii)

... the season of all natures, sleep.
                Macbeth (III, iv)

HEALTH

*O, thou invisible spirit of wine, if thou hast no name
to be known by, let us call thee devil!*
Othello (II, iii)

We are merely cheated of our lives by drunkards.
The Tempest (I, i)

'Scape being drunk for want of wine...
The Tempest (II, i)

*... they were red-hot with drinking;
So full of valour that they smote the air
For breathing in their faces; beat the ground
For kissing of their feet; yet always bending
Towards their project.*
The Tempest (IV, i)

Olivia: *What's a drunken man like, fool?*
Clown: *Like a drowned man, a fool, and a
madman: one draught above heat makes
him a fool; the second mads him; and a
third drowns him.*
Twelfth Night (I, v)

HONESTY

> . . . *the honour of a maid is her name;*
> *And no legacy is so rich as honesty.*
> *All's Well That Ends Well (III, v)*

> [word. . .
> *I would not buy their mercy at the price of one fair*
> *Coriolanus (III, iii)*

> *But if I were as wise as honest, then*
> *My purpose would prove well.*
> *Cymbeline (III, iv)*

> . . . *to lapse in fulness is sorer than to lie for need;*
> . . . *and falsehood is worse in kings than beggars.*
> *Cymbeline (III, vi)*

> *This above all,—to thine ownself be true;*
> *And it must follow, as the night the day,*
> *Thou canst not then be false to any man.*
> *Hamlet (I, iii)*

> . . . *to be honest, as this world goes,*
> *Is to be one man picked out of ten thousand.*
> *Hamlet (II, ii)*

> *Could beauty, my lord,*
> *Have better commerce than with honesty?*
> *Hamlet (III, i)*

> . . . *men may construe things after their fashion,*
> *Clean from the purpose of the things themselves.*
> *Julius Caesar (I, iii)*

> *There is no terror, Cassius, in your threats,*
> *For I am armed so strong in honesty*
> *That they pass by me as the idle wind.*
> *Julius Caesar (IV, iii)*

HONESTY

> ... *your words,*
> *Domestics to you, serve your will as 't please*
> *Yourself pronounce their office.*
> *King Henry VIII (II, iv)*

> *Get thee glass eyes*
> *And, like a scurvy politician, seem*
> *To see the things thou dost not.*
> *King Lear (IV, vi)*

> *Where I could not be honest, I never yet was valiant.*
> *King Lear (V, i)*

> *Speak what we feel, not what we ought to say.*
> *King Lear (V, iii)*

> *How God, and good men, hate so foul a liar.*
> *King Richard II (I, i)*

> *... he was ever precise in promise-keeping.*
> *Measure for Measure (I, ii)*

> *It oft falls out,* [mean.
> *To have what we would have, we speak not what we*
> *Measure for Measure (II, iv)*

> *I have no tongue but one.*
> *Measure for Measure (II, iv)*

> *I do despise a liar as I do despise one that is false;*
> *or, as I despise one that is not true.*
> *Merry Wives of Windsor (I, i)*

> *I'll take thy word for faith, not ask thine oath;*
> *Who shuns not to break one, will sure crack both.*
> *Pericles (I, ii)*

HONESTY

I believe you;
Your honour and your goodness teach me to't,
Without your vows.
     Pericles (III, iii)

Falseness cannot come from thee, for thou look'st
Modest as Justice, and thou seem'st a palace
For the crown'd Truth to dwell in:
I will believe thee.
     Pericles (V, i)

When we for recompense have praised the vile,
It stains the glory in that happy verse
Which aptly sings the good.
     Timon of Athens (I, i)

First Lord: What time o'day is 't. . . ?
Apemantus: Time to be honest.
     Timon of Athens (I, i)

Believe me, I speak as my understanding instructs me,
And as mine honesty puts it to utterance.
     Winter's Tale (I, i)

Since what I am to say must be but that
Which contradicts my accusation, and
The testimony on my part no other
But what comes from myself, it shall scarce boot me
To say, <u>Not guilty</u>*; mine integrity,*
Being counted falsehood, shall, as I express it,
Be so receiv'd. But thus, if powers divine
Behold our human actions—as they do,—
I doubt not, then, but innocence shall make
False accusation blush, and tyranny
Tremble at patience.—
     Winter's Tale (III, ii)

HONOR

. . . have hearts
Inclinable to honour. . .
Coriolanus (II, ii)

Your dishonour
Mangles true judgement and bereaves the state
Of that integrity which should become't,
Not having the power to do the good it would
For the ill which doth control 't.
Coriolanus (III, i)

Breaking his oath and resolution like
A twist of rotten silk. . .
Coriolanus (V, vi)

To-day how many would have given their honours
To have sav'd their carcases? took heel to do't
And yet died too!
Cymbeline (V, iii)

...I love the name of honour more than I fear death.
Julius Caesar (I, ii)

Love they to live, that love and honour have.
King Richard II (V, iii)

And he shall spend mine honour with his shame,
As thriftless sons their scraping father's gold.
King Richard II (V, iii)

Let none presume
To wear an undeserved dignity.
Oh, that estates, degrees, and offices
Were not derived corruptly, and that clear honour
Were purchased by the merit of the wearer!
Merchant of Venice (II, ix)

HONOR

I rather will suspect the sun with cold
Than thee with wantonness,
Now doth thine honour stand...
As firm as faith.
                      Merry Wives of Windsor (IV, iv)

My actions are as noble as my thoughts,
That never relish'd of a base descent.
I came unto your court for honour's cause...
                      Pericles (II, v)

There is no time so miserable but a man may be true.
                      Timon of Athens (IV, iii)

Give me a staff of honour for mine age,
But not a sceptre to control the world...
                      Titus Andronicus (I, i)

Have you not set mine honour at the stake?
                      Twelfth Night (III, i)

His words are bonds, his oaths are oracles;
His love sincere, his thoughts immaculate;
His tears, pure messengers sent from his heart;
His heart as far from fraud as heaven from earth.
                      Two Gentlemen of Verona (II, vii)

HOPE

And hope to enjoy, is little less in joy,
Than hope enjoy'd.
>*King Richard II (II, ii)*

True hope is swift, and flies with swallow's wings,
Kings it makes gods, and meaner creatures kings.
>*King Richard II (V, ii)*

Now is the winter of our discontent
Made glorious summer. . .
>*King Richard III (I, i)*

The miserable have no other medicine
But only hope.
>*Measure for Measure (III, i)*

. . . entertain him with hope. . .
>*Merry Wives of Windsor (II, i)*

Night's candles are burnt out, and jocund day
Stands tiptoe on the misty mountaintops.
>*Romeo and Juliet (III, v)*

. . . and let not discontent
Daunt all your hopes. . .
>*Titus Andronicus (I, i)*

I have been troubled in my sleep this night,
But dawning day new comfort hath inspir'd.
>*Titus Andronicus (II, ii)*

Hope is a lover's staff; walk hence with that,
And manage it against despairing thoughts.
>*Two Gentlemen of Verona (III, i)*

HUMILITY

In nature's infinite book of secrecy,
A little I can read.
>*Antony and Cleopatra (I, ii)*

I . . . am not
Of stronger earth than others.
>*Coriolanus (V, iii)*

Take each man's censure, but reserve thy judgment.
>*Hamlet (I, iii)*

Then you lost
The view of earthly glory.
>*King Henry VIII (I, i)*

Have more than thou showest,
Speak less than thou knowest,
Lend less than thou owest,
Ride more than thou goest,
Learn more than thou trowest (know)...
>*King Lear (I, iv)*

Nothing almost sees miracles
But misery.
>*King Lear (II, ii)*

I love the people,
But do not like to stage me to their eyes.
Though it do well, I do not relish well
Their loud applause and Aves vehement,
Nor do I think the man of safe discretion
That does affect it.
>*Measure for Measure (I, i)*

HUMILITY

A city on whom plenty held full hand,
For riches strew'd herself even in the streets;
Whose towers bore heads so high they kiss'd the clouds,
And strangers ne'er beheld, but wonder'd at;
Whose men and dames so jetted and adorn'd,
Like one another's glass to trim them by:
Their tables were stor'd full, to glad the sight,
And not so much to feed on, as delight;
All poverty was scorn'd, and pride so great,
The name of help grew odious to repeat. . .
But see what heaven can do! By this our change,
These mouths, whom but of late, earth, sea, and air
Were all too little to content and please,
Although they gave their creatures in abundance,
As houses are defil'd for want of use,
They are now starv'd for want of exercise:
Those palates who, not yet two summers younger,
Must have invention to delight the taste,
Would now be glad of bread, and beg for it. . .
            Pericles (I, iv)

What I have been, I have forgot to know;
But what I am, want teaches me to think on.
            Pericles (II, i)

I have no more doublets than backs, no more stockings than legs, nor no more shoes than feet; nay, sometime more feet than shoes, or such shoes as my toes look through the overleather.
            Taming of the Shrew (induction)

HYPOCRISY

You do not know him, my lord, as we do: certain it is, that he will steal himself into a man's favour, and, for a week, escape a great deal of discoveries; but when you find him out, you have him ever after . . . when his disguise and he is parted, tell me what a sprat you shall find him. . .
All's Well That Ends Well (III, vi)

Do not, as some ungracious pastors do,
Show me the steep and thorny way to heaven;
Whilst, like a puff'd and reckless libertine,
Himself the primrose path of dalliance treads,
And recks not his own rede (advice).
Hamlet (I, iii)

Breathing like sanctified and pious bonds,
The better to beguile.
Hamlet (I, iii)

That one may smile, and smile, and be a villain. . .
Hamlet (I, v)

. . . the devil hath power
To assume a pleasing shape. . .
Hamlet (II, ii)

. . . there is a kind of confession in your looks, which your modesties have not craft enough to colour. . .
Hamlet (II, ii)

'Tis too much prov'd,—that, with devotion's visage,
And pious action, we do sugar o'er
The devil himself.
Hamlet (III, i)

HYPOCRISY

Or are you like the painting of a sorrow,
A face without a heart?
            Hamlet (IV, vii)

. . . some that smile have in their hearts. . .
Millions of mischiefs.
            Julius Caesar (IV, i)

But out upon this half-fac'd fellowship!
            King Henry IV, Part I (I, iii)

            . . . but now the bishop
Turns insurrection to religion,
Suppos'd sincere and holy in his thoughts. . .
            King Henry IV, Part II (I, i)

. . . I am well acquainted with your manner of
wrenching the true cause the false way.
            King Henry IV, Part II (II, i)

That you should seal this lawless bloody book
Of forg'd rebellion with a seal divine,
And consecrate commotion's bitter edge?
            King Henry IV, Part II (IV, i)

            Who hath not heard it spoken,
How deep you were within the books of God? . . .
To us, the imagin'd voice of heaven itself.
The very opener, and intelligencer,
Between the grace, the sanctities of heaven,
And our dull workings. O, who shall believe,
But you misuse the reverence of your place;
Employ the countenance and grace of heaven. . .
In deeds dishonourable? You have taken up,
Under the counterfeited seal of God.
            King Henry IV, Part II (IV, ii)

HYPOCRISY

Thou, that giv'st whores indulgences to sin. . .
. . . thou wolf in sheep's array.—
Out, tawny-coats!—out, scarlet hypocrite!
                King Henry VI, Part I (I, iii)

Stay, my lord legate; you shall first receive
The sum of money which I promised
Should be deliver'd to his holiness
For clothing me in these grave ornaments (holy
       attire).
                King Henry VI, Part I (V, i)

Smooth runs the water where the brook is deep,
And in his simple show he harbours treason,
The fox barks not when he would steal the lamb,
No, no, my sovereign; Gloster is a man
Unsounded yet, and full of deep deceit. . .
Seems he a dove? his feathers are but borrow'd,
For he's disposed as the hateful raven.
Is he a lamb? his skin is surely lent him,
For he's inclin'd as is the ravenous wolf.
Who cannot steal a shape that means deceit?
                King Henry VI, Part II (III, i)

Hide not thy poison with such sugar'd words.
                King Henry VI, Part II (III, ii)

              You're meek and humble mouthed.
You sign your place and calling, in full seeming,
With meekness and humility, but your heart
Is crammed with arrogancy, spleen, and pride.
                King Henry VIII (II, iv)

They should be good men; their affairs as righteous:
But all hoods make not monks.
                King Henry VIII (III, i)

HYPOCRISY

Ye have angels' faces,
But Heaven knows your hearts.
    King Henry VIII (III, i)

You have beguil'd me with a counterfeit,
Resembling majesty; which, being touch'd, and tried,
Proves valueless.
    King John (III, i)

Time shall unfold what plaited cunning hides.
Who cover faults, at last shame them derides.
    King Lear (I, i)

Anne: I would I knew thy heart.
Glo: 'Tis figur'd in my tongue.
Anne: I fear me both are false.
    King Richard III (I, ii)

I do the wrong, and first begin to brawl.
The secret mischiefs that I set abroach
I lay unto the grievous charge of others. . .
But then I sigh, and, with a piece of scripture,
Tell them that God bids us do good for evil:
And thus I clothe my naked villainy
With old odd ends, stol'n out of holy writ;
And seem a saint, when most I play the devil.—
    King Richard III (I, iii)

Hast thou that holy feeling in thy soul,
To counsel me to make my peace with God,
And art thou yet to your own soul so blind,
That thou wilt war with God by murdering me?
    King Richard III (I, iv)

HYPOCRISY

Take heed you dally not before your king,
Lest he, that is the supreme King of kings,
Confound your hidden falsehood...
    King Richard III (II, i)

An, that deceit should steal such gentle shape,
And with a virtuous vizor hide foul guile!
He is my son, ay, and therein my shame,
Yet from my dugs he drew not this deceit.
    King Richard III (II, ii)

Nor God, nor I, delights in perjur'd men.
    Love's Labour's Lost (V, ii)

To hide deceit, and give the harmless show:
An humble gait, calm looks, eyes wailing still...
But, like a constant and confirmed devil,
He entertain'd a show so seeming just,
And therein so ensconc'd his secret evil,
That jealousy itself could not mistrust
False-creeping craft and perjury should thrust
 Into so bright a day such black-fac'd storms,
 Or blot with hell-born sin such saint-like forms.
    Lucrece (stanzas 216, 217)

To me came Tarquin armed; so beguil'd
With outward honesty, but yet defil'd
 With inward vice...
    Lucrece (stanza 221)

And oftentimes, to win us to our harm,
The instruments of darkness tell us truths,
Win us with honest trifles, to betray's
In deepest consequence.
    Macbeth (I, iii)

HYPOCRISY

False face must hide what the false heart doth know.
   Macbeth (I, vii)

To show an unfelt sorrow is an office
Which the false man does easy.
   Macbeth (II, iii)

Thieves for their robbery have authority
When judges steal themselves.
   Measure for Measure (II, ii)

O place! O form! How often dost thou
With thy case, thy habit, wrench awe from foes,
And tie the wiser souls to thy false seeming!
   Measure for Measure (II, iv)

      Oh, perilous mouths,
That bear in them one and the selfsame tongue,
Either of condemnation or approof,
Bidding the law make curtsy to their will,
Hooking both right and wrong to the appetite,
To follow as it draws!
   Measure for Measure (II, iv)

That we were all, as some would seem to be,
From our faults, as faults from seeming, free!
   Measure for Measure (III, ii)

There are a sort of men whose visages
Do cream and mantle like a standing pond,
And do a willful stillness entertain,
With purpose to be dressed in an opinion
Of wisdom, gravity, profound conceit . . . when. . .
If they should speak, would almost damn those ears
Which, hearing them, would call their brothers fools.
   Merchant of Venice (I, i)

HYPOCRISY

The Devil can cite Scripture for his purpose.
And evil soul producing holy witness
Is like a villain with a smiling cheek,
A goodly apple rotten at the heart.
Oh, what a goodly outside falsehood hath!
          Merchant of Venice (I, iii)

By the fool multitude, that choose by show,
Not learning more than the fond eye doth teach,
Which pries not to the interior but. . .
Builds in the weather on the outward wall. . .
          Merchant of Venice (II, ix)

So may the outward shows be least themselves.
The world is still deceived with ornament.
In law, what plea so tainted and corrupt
But, being seasoned with a gracious voice,
Obscures the show of evil?
          Merchant of Venice (III, ii)

Thus ornament is but the guiled shore
To a most dangerous sea. . .
The seeming truth which cunning times put on
To entrap the wisest.
          Merchant of Venice (III, ii)

. . . the heresies that men do leave,
Are hated most of those they did deceive. . .
          Midsummer Night's Dream (II, ii)

Though I do hate him as I do hell-pains,
Yet, for necessity of present life,
I must show out a flag and sign of love,
Which is indeed but sign.
          Othello (I, i)

HYPOCRISY

[He] thinks men honest that but seem to be so;
And will as tenderly be led by the nose
As asses are.
            Othello (I, iii)

                    . . . if thou hast eyes to see;
She has deceiv'd her father, and may thee.
            Othello (I, iii)

When devils will the blackest sins put on,
They do suggest at first with heavenly shows. . .
            Othello (II, iii)

Faith, I have heard too much; for your words and
performances are no kin together.
            Othello (IV, ii)

How courtesy would seem to cover sin,
When what is done is like an hypocrite,
The which is good in nothing but in sight!
            Pericles (I, i)

Who makes the fairest show means most deceit.
            Pericles (I, iv)

Oh, serpent heart, hid with a flowering face!
            Romeo and Juliet (III, ii)

How many lambs might the stern wolf betray,
If like a lamb he could his looks translate!
            Sonnet XCVI

For I have sworn thee fair, and thought thee bright,
Who art as black as hell, as dark as night.
            Sonnet CXLVII

HYPOCRISY

. . . they durst not . . . set. . .
A mark so bloody on the business; but
With colours fairer painted their foul ends.
The Tempest (I, ii)

. . . two voices; a most
delicate monster! His forward voice now, is to speak
well of his friend; his backward voice is to utter foul
speeches and to detract.
The Tempest (II, ii)

You undergo too strict a paradox,
Striving to make an ugly deed look fair. . .
You cannot make gross sins look clear.
Timon of Athens (III, v)

O cruel, irreligious piety!
Titus Andronicus (I, i)

Thou subtle, perjur'd, false, disloyal man!
Think'st thou, I am so shallow, so conceitless,
To be seduced by thy flattery,
That hast deceiv'd so many with thy vows?
Two Gentlemen of Verona (IV, ii)

Alas . . . thou hast entertain'd
A fox, to be the shepherd of thy lambs. . .
Two Gentlemen of Verona (IV, iv)

I am sorry I must never trust thee more,
But count the world a stranger for thy sake.
The private wound is deepest: O time most accurs'd!
'Mongst all foes, that a friend should be the worst.
Two Gentlemen of Verona (V, iv)

IMMORTALITY

> . . . *all that lives must die,*
> *Passing through nature to eternity.*
> *Hamlet (I, ii)*

God knows whether those....shall inherit his kingdom...
King Henry IV, Part II (II, ii)

> *Tarry, dear cousin Suffolk!*
> *My soul shall thine keep company to heaven.*
> *Tarry, sweet soul, for mine, then fly a-breast...*
> *King Henry V (IV, vi)*

Come, side by side together live and die;
And soul with soul from France to heaven fly.
King Henry VI, Part I (IV, v)

Thou setter-up and plucker-down of kings,—
Beseeching thee, if with thy will it stands,
That to my foes this body must be prey,—
Yet that thy brazen gates of heaven may ope,
And give sweet passage to my sinful soul!—
Now, lords, take leave until we meet again,
Where'er it be, in heaven or in earth.
King Henry VI, Part III (II, iii)

Then God forgive the sin of all those souls,
That to their everlasting residence,
Before the dew of evening fall, shall fleet...
King John (II, i)

> . . . *I have heard you say,*
> *That we shall see and know our friends in heaven...*
> *And so he'll die: and, rising so again,*
> *When I shall meet him in the court of heaven...*
> *King John (III, iv)*

IMMORTALITY

Heaven take my soul...
    King John (IV, iii)

The life, the right, and truth of all this realm
Is fled to heaven...
    King John (IV, iii)

My comfort is, that heaven will take our souls...
    King Richard II (III, i)

      ... [He] gave
His body to that pleasant country's earth,
And his pure soul unto his captain Christ,
Under whose colours he had fought so long...
Sweet peace conduct his sweet soul to the bosom
Of good old Abraham! ...
    King Richard II (IV, i)

Our holy lives must win a new world's crown...
    King Richard II (V, i)

I every day expect an embassage
From my Redeemer to redeem me hence;
And now in peace my soul shall part to heaven...
    King Richard III (II, i)

Olivia: I know his soul is in heaven, fool.
Clown: The more fool, madonna, to mourn for your
    brother's soul being in heaven.
    Twelfth Night (I, v)

INFLUENCE

In time we hate that which we often fear.
Antony and Cleopatra (I, iii)

Scar: *I never saw an action of such shame;*
Experience, manhood, honour, ne'er before
Did violate so itself...
Ant: *I have offended reputation,—*
A most unnoble swerving...
See how I convey my shame out of thine eye
By looking back what I have left behind
'Stroy'd in dishonour.
Cleo: *O, my lord, my lord!*
Forgive my fearful sails! I little thought
You would have follow'd.
Ant: *Egypt, thou knew'st too well   [strings.*
My heart was to thy rudder tied by the
And thou shoulds't tow me after. [knewest.
O'er my spirit thy full supremacy thou
And that thy beck might—from the bidding
Of the Gods—command me.
Cleo: *O, my pardon!*
Antony and Cleopatra (III, xi)

My friends, the boy hath taught us manly duties.
Cymbeline (IV, ii)

Company, villainous company,
Hath been the spoil of me.
King Henry IV, Part I (III, iii)

It is certain, that either wise bearing, or ignorant carriage, is caught, as men take diseases, one of another; and therefore, let men take heed of their company.
King Henry IV, Part II (V, i)

INFLUENCE

The love of wicked friends converts to fear,
That fear to hate; and hate turns one, or both,
To worthy danger, and deserved death.
     King Richard II (V, i)

Who can impress the forest, bid the tree
Unfix his earthbound root?
     Macbeth (IV, i)

       Pause a while,
And let my counsel sway you in this cause.
     Much Ado About Nothing (IV, i)

They'll take suggestion as a cat laps milk.
     The Tempest (II, i)

A fiend like thee might bear my soul to hell!
     Twelfth Night (III, iv)

I like thy counsel; well hast thou advis'd:
And, that thou mayst perceive how well I like it,
The execution of it shall make known:
Even with the speediest expedition. . .
     Two Gentlemen of Verona (I, iii)

You, that are thus so tender o'er his follies,
Will never do him good, not one of you.
     Winter's Tale (II, iii)

INNOCENCE

. . . neither having the accent of Christians, nor the gait of Christian. . .

Hamlet (III, ii)

A heart unspotted is not easily daunted.

King Henry VI, Part II (III, i)

What stronger breast-plate than a heart untainted!
Thrice is he arm'd, that hath his quarrel just;
And he but naked, though lock'd up in steel,
Whose conscience with injustice is corrupted.

King Henry VI, Part II (III, ii)

This earthly saint, adored by this devil,
Little suspecteth the false worshipper;
For unstain'd thoughts do seldom dream on evil;
Birds never lim'd no secret bushes fear:
So guiltless she securely gives good cheer
  And reverend welcome to her princely guest,
  Whose inward ill no outward harm express'd. . .

Lucrece (stanza 13)

And my true eyes have never practis'd how
To cloak offences with a cunning brow.

Lucrece (stanza 107)

For we are soft as our complexions are,
And credulous to false prints.

Measure for Measure (II, iv)

The silence often of pure innocence
Persuades, when speaking fails.

Winter's Tale (II, ii)

JUDGMENT

What he cannot help in his nature, you account a vice in him.
     Coriolanus (I, i)

No reckoning made, but sent to my account
With all my imperfections on my head:
O, horrible! O, horrible! Most horrible!
     Hamlet (I, v)

Priest: She should in ground unsanctified have lodg'd
   Till the last trumpet. . .
Laer: . . . I tell thee churlish priest,
   A minist'ring angel shall my sister be,
   When thou liest howling.
     Hamlet (V, i)

. . . awake your senses, that you may the better judge.
     Julius Caesar (III, ii)

O judgment, thou art fled to brutish beasts,
And men have lost their reason!
     Julius Caesar (III, ii)

Brutus: I do not like your faults.
Cassius: A friendly eye could never see such faults.
     Julius Caesar (IV, iii)

O thou that judgest all things, stay my thoughts! . . .
If my suspect be false, forgive me, God;
For judgment only doth belong to thee!
     King Henry VI, Part II (III, ii)

Forbear to judge, for we are sinners all.
     King Henry VI, Part II (III, iii)

JUDGMENT

*From that supernal Judge that stirs good thoughts
In any breast of strong authority,
To look into the blots and stains of right...
Under whose warrant, I impeach thy wrong,
And by whose help, I mean to chastise it.*
   King John (II, i)

*O, when the last account 'twixt heaven and earth
Is to be made, then shall this hand and seal
Witness against us to damnation!*
   King John (IV, ii)

*Why, all the souls that were forfeit once,
And He that might the vantage best have took
Found out the remedy. How would you be
If He, which is the top of judgment, should
But judge you as you are? Oh, think on that,
And mercy then will breathe within your lips,
Like man new-made.*
   Measure for Measure (II, ii)

                    *Go to your bosom,
Knock there, and ask your heart what it doth know
That's like my brother's fault.*
   Measure for Measure (II, ii)

*Shame to him whose cruel striking
Kills for faults of his own liking!*
   Measure for Measure (III, ii)

JUSTICE

Was there ever any man thus beaten out of season,
When in the why and the wherefore is neither rhyme
nor reason?
> *Comedy of Errors (II, ii)*

'Tis greater skill
In a true hate, to pray they have their will:
The very devils cannot plague them better.
> *Cymbeline (II, v)*

In the corrupted currents of this world,
Offence's gilded hand may shove by justice;
And oft 'tis seen the wicked prize itself
Buys out the law: but 'tis not so above...
> *Hamlet (III, iii)*

And where the offence is, let the great axe fall.
> *Hamlet (IV, v)*

You have conspir'd against our royal person,
Join'd with an enemy proclaim'd and from his coffers
Receiv'd the golden earnest of our death;
Wherein you would have sold your king to slaughter,
His princes and his peers to servitude,
His subects to oppression and contempt,
And his whole kingdom into desolation.
Touching our person, seek we no revenge;
But we our kingdom's safety must so tender,
Whose ruin you have sought, that to her laws
We do deliver you. Get you therefore hence,
Poor miserable wretches, to your death:
The taste whereof, God, of his mercy, give
You patience to endure, and true repentance
Of all your dear offences!
> *King Henry V (II, ii)*

JUSTICE

*Now, if these men have defeated the law, and outrun
native punishment, though they can outstrip men, they
have no wings to fly from God.*
King Henry V (IV, i)

*For what doth cherish weeds but gentle air?
And what makes robbers bold but too much lenity?*
King Henry VI, Part III (II, vi)

*For though usurpers sway the rule awhile,
Yet heavens are just, and time suppresseth wrongs.*
King Henry VI, Part III (III, iii)

*A little fire is quickly trodden out,
Which being suffer'd, rivers cannot quench.*
King Henry VI, Part III (IV, viii)

*Through tattered clothes small vices do appear,
Robes and furred gowns hide all. Plate sin with gold
And the strong lance of justice hurtless breaks.
Arm it in rags, a pigmy's straw does pierce it.*
King Lear (IV, vi)

*Rage must be withstood:
Give me his gage:—lions make leopards tame.*
King Richard II (I, i)

*Put we our quarrel to the will of heaven;
Who when they see the hours ripe on earth,
Will rain hot vengeance on offenders' heads. . .
Let heaven revenge. . .*
King Richard II (I, ii)

*. . . then, if angels fight,
Weak men must fall, for heaven still guards the right.*
King Richard II (III, ii)

JUSTICE

If thou do pardon, whosoever pray,
More sins, for this forgiveness, prosper may.
This fester'd joint cut off, the rest rests sound;
This, let alone, will all the rest confound.
     King Richard II (V, iii)

Erroneous vassal! the great King of kings
Hath in the table of his law commanded
That thou shalt do no murder...
Take heed; for he holds vengeance in his hand,
To hurl upon their heads that break his law.
     King Richard III (I, iv)

That high All-seer which I dallied with,
Hath turn'd my feigned prayer on my head,
And given in earnest what I begg'd in jest.
Thus doth he force the swords of wicked men
To turn their own points on their masters' bosom...
     King Richard III (V, i)

Why should the private pleasure of some one
Become the public plague of many more?
Let sin, alone committed, light alone
Upon his head that hath transgressed so;
Let guiltless souls be freed from guilty woe;
For one's offense why should so many fall,
To plague a private sin in general? ...
And one man's lust these many lives confound...
     Lucrece (stanzas 212, 213)

    ... suppose thou dost defend me
From what is past; the help that thou shalt lend me
Comes all too late, yet let the traitor die;
For sparing justice feeds iniquity.
     Lucrece (stanza 241)

JUSTICE

We still have judgement here, that we but teach
Bloody instructions, which being taught return
To plague the inventor. This even-handed justice
Commends the ingredients of our poisoned chalice
To our own lips.
              Macbeth (I, vii)

                  . . . for though
This king were great, his greatness was no guard
To bar heav'ns shaft, but sin had his reward.
            Pericles (II, iv)

KINDNESS

Forbear sharp speeches to her; she's a lady
So tender of rebukes, that words are strokes,
And strokes death to her.
           Cymbeline (III, v)

           ... for when a world of men
Could not prevail with all their oratory,
Yet hath a woman's kindness over-rul'd...
           King Henry VI, Part I (II, ii)

                A kind heart he hath,—
A woman would run through fire and water
For such a kind heart.
           Merry Wives of Windsor (III, iv)

And woo her with some spirit when she comes.
Say that she rail; why, then I'll tell her plain
She sings as sweetly as a nightingale.
Say that she frown; I'll say she looks as clear
As morning roses newly washed with dew.
           Taming of the Shrew (II, i)

This is a way to kill a wife with kindness...
           Taming of the Shrew (IV, i)

Timon will to the woods, where he shall find
The unkindest beast more kinder than mankind.
           Timon of Athens (IV, i)

... there is ... no railing in a known discreet man,
though he do nothing but reprove.
           Twelfth Night (I, v)

... my bosom is full of kindness; and I am yet so
near the manners of my mother...
           Twelfth Night (II, i)

KNOWLEDGE

>   . . . *all the learnings that his time*
> *Could make him the receiver of . . . he took. . .*
> *As we do air, fast as 't was minister'd,*
> *And in 's spring became a harvest. . .*
> *A sample to the youngest.*
> >   *Cymbeline (I, i)*

There are more things in heaven and earth. . .
Than are dreamt of in your philosophy.
>   *Hamlet (I, v)*

If to do were as easy as to know what were good to do, chapels had been churches, and poor men's cottages princes' palaces. It is a good divine that follows his own instruction: I can easier teach twenty what were good to be done, than be one of the twenty to follow mine own teaching.
>   *Merchant of Venice (I, ii)*

Oh, what learning is!
>   *Romeo and Juliet (III, iii)*

My library was dukedom large enough.
>   *The Tempest (I, ii)*

And as the morning steals upon the night,
Melting the darkness, so their rising senses
Begin to chase the ignorant fumes that mantle
Their clearer reason . . . their understanding
Begins to swell; and the approaching tide
Will shortly fill the reasonable shore,
That now lies foul and muddy.
>   *The Tempest (V, i)*

KNOWLEDGE

Things growing are not ripe until their season.
So I, being young, till now ripe not to reason;
And touching now the point of human skill,
Reason becomes the marshal to my will...
                Midsummer Night's Dream (II, ii)

Our own precedent passions do instruct us
What levity's in youth.
           Timon of Athens (I, i)

... when wit and youth is come to harvest,
Your wife is like to reap a proper man...
           Twelfth Night (III, i)

I say, there is no darkness but ignorance...
           Twelfth Night (IV, ii)

I rather would entreat thy company,
To see the wonders of the world abroad,
Than, living dully sluggardiz'd at home,
Wear out thy youth with shapeless idleness.
           Two Gentlemen of Verona (I, i)

     ... he cannot be a perfect man,
Not being try'd and tutor'd in the world:
Experience is by industry achiev'd,
And perfected by the swift course of time...
           Two Gentlemen of Verona (I, iii)

... the behaviour of the young gentleman gives him
out to be of good capacity and breeding...
           Twelfth Night (III, iv)

Verily, I speak it in the freedom of my knowledge.
           Winter's Tale (I, i)

LAW

Our Ancestor...
Ordain'd our laws,—whose use the sword of Caesar
Hath too much mangled; whose repair and franchise
Shall, by the power we hold, be our good deed.
    Cymbeline (III, i)

... nature must obey necessity...
    Julius Caesar (IV, iii)

We have strict statutes and most biting laws,
The needful bits and curbs to headstrong steeds...
    Measure for Measure (I, iii)

We must not make a scarecrow of the law,
Setting it up to fear the birds of prey,
And let it keep one shape till custom make it
Their perch, and not their terror.
    Measure for Measure (II, i)

There is a law in each well-order'd nation,
To curb those raging appetites that are
Most disobedient and refractory.
    Troilus and Cressida (II, ii)

LEADERSHIP

. . . when two authorities are up,
Neither supreme, how soon confusion
May enter 'twixt the gap of both. . .
            Coriolanus (III, i)

Keep Rome in safety, and chairs of justice
Supplied with worthy men! Plant love among 's!
            Coriolanus (III, iii)

The people will remain uncertain whilst
'Twixt you there's difference. . .
            Coriolanus (V, vi)

The abuse of greatness is when it disjoins
Remorse from power. . .
That lowliness is young ambition's ladder,
Whereto the climber-upward turns his face.
But when he once attains the upmost round,
He then unto the ladder turns his back,
Looks in the clouds, scorning the base degrees
By which he did ascend.
            Julius Caesar (II, i)

Gives not the hawthorn-bush a sweeter shade
To shepherds, looking on their silly sheep,
Than doth a rich embroider'd canopy
To kings, that fear their subjects' treachery?
O, yes, it doth; a thousand fold, it doth!
And to conclude,—the shepherds, homely curds,
His cold thin drink out of his leather bottle,
His wonted sleep under a fresh tree's shade,
All which secure and sweetly he enjoys,
Is far beyond a prince's delicates,
His viands sparkling in a golden cup. . .
When care, mistrust, and treason wait on him.
            King Henry VI, Part III (II, v)

LEADERSHIP

I have not stopp'd mine ears to their demands,
Nor posted off their suits with slow delays;
My pity hath been balm to heal their wounds,
My mildness hath allay'd their swelling griefs,
My mercy dried their water-flowing tears;
I have not been desirous of their wealth,
Nor much oppress'd them with great subsidies,
Nor forward of revenge, though they much err'd...
    King Henry VI, Part III (IV, viii)

Corruption wins not more than honesty.
Still in thy right hand carry gentle peace...
Be just... Let all the ends thou aim'st at
Be thy country's, thy God's and truth's.
    King Henry VIII (III, ii)

You taught me how to know the face of right...
    King John (V, ii)

        How in one house
Should many people under two commands
Hold amity? 'Tis hard, almost impossible.
    King Lear (II, iv)

'Tis the times' plague when madmen lead the blind.
    King Lear (IV, i)

Princes have but their titles for their glories,
An outward honour for an inward toil;
And, for unfelt imagination,
They often feel a world of restless cares;
So that, between their titles and low name,
There's nothing differs but the outward fame.
    King Richard III (I, iv)

LEADERSHIP

Hence shall we see,
If power change purpose, what our seemers be.
Measure for Measure (I, iii)

He who the sword of Heaven will bear
Should be as holy as severe,
Pattern in himself to know,
Grace to stand and virtue go,
More nor less to others paying
Than by self-offenses weighing.
Measure for Measure (III, ii)

They do abuse the king that flatter him:
For flattery is the bellows blows up sin;
The thing the which is flatter'd, but a spark,
To which that blast gives heat and stronger glowing;
Whereas reproof, obedient and in order,
Fits kings as they are men, for they may err.
Pericles (I, ii)

The noblest mind he carries
That ever governed man.
Timon of Athens (I, i)

Indeed a sheep doth very often stray,
An if the shepherd be awhile away.
Two Gentlemen of Verona (I, i)

LOVE

The time was once when thou unurged wouldst vow
That never words were music to thine ear,
That never object pleasing in thine eye,
That never touch well welcome to thy hand,
That never meat sweet-savored in thy taste,
Unless I spake, or looked, or touched, or carved to
thee.
     Comedy of Errors (II, ii)

She's so conjunctive to my life and soul,
That, as the star moves not but in his sphere,
I could not but by her.
     Hamlet (IV, vii)

There lives within the very flame of love
A kind of wick or snuff that will abate it...
     Hamlet (IV, vii)

Thy life did manifest, thou lov'dst me not...
     King Henry IV, Part II (IV, iv)

     Love's not love
When it is mingled with regards that stand
Aloof from the entire point.
     King Lear (I, i)

My love should kindle to inflamed respect.
     King Lear (I, i)

Love talks with better knowledge, and knowledge with
dearer love.
     Measure for Measure (III, ii)

... love is blind, and lovers cannot see
The pretty follies that themselves commit...
     Merchant of Venice (II, vi)

LOVE

You see me . . . where I stand,
Such as I am. Though for myself alone
I would not be ambitious in my wish,
To wish myself much better; yet for you
I would be trebled twenty times myself—
A thousand times more fair, ten thousand times
More rich—
That only to stand high in your account,
I might in virtues, beauties, livings, friends,
Exceed account.
                    Merchant of Venice (III, ii)

O powerful love! that, in some respects, makes a beast a man; in some other, a man a beast.
                    Merry Wives of Windsor (V, v)

. . . therefore is Love said to be a child,
Because in choice he is so oft beguiled.
                    Midsummer Night's Dream (I, i)

. . . for aught that I could ever read,
Could ever hear by tale or history,
The course of true love never did run smooth. . .
                    Midsummer Night's Dream (I, i)

Love can transpose to form and dignity.
Love looks not with the eyes, but with the mind. . .
                    Midsummer Night's Dream (I, i)

. . . reason and love keep little company together nowadays. . .
                    Midsummer Night's Dream (III, i)

What, can you do me greater harm than hate?
                    Midsummer Night's Dream (III, ii)

LOVE

Love is a smoke raised with the fume of sighs;
Being purged, a fire sparkling in lovers' eyes;
Being vexed, a sea nourished with lovers' tears.
What is it else? A madness most discreet,
A choking gall and a preserving sweet.
                    Romeo and Juliet (I, i)

Is love a tender thing?
              Romeo and Juliet (I, iv)

Did my heart love till now?
               Romeo and Juliet (I, v)

If love be blind, love cannot hit the mark.
               Romeo and Juliet (II, i)

. . . stony limits cannot hold love out.
And what love can do, that dares love attempt. . .
              Romeo and Juliet (II, ii)

This bud of love, by summer's ripening breath,
May prove a beauteous flower. . .
              Romeo and Juliet (II, ii)

My bounty is as boundless as the sea,
My love as deep; the more I give to thee,
The more I have, for both are infinite.
               Romeo and Juliet (II, ii)

Young men's love then lies
Not truly in their hearts, but in their eyes.
             Romeo and Juliet (II, iii)

. . . a fool's paradise. . .
              Romeo and Juliet (II, iv)

LOVE

. . . love moderately, long love doth so,
Too swift arrives as tardy as too slow.
Romeo and Juliet (II, vi)

. . . if love be blind,
It best agrees with night.
Romeo and Juliet (III, ii)

See what a scourge is laid upon your hate
That Heaven finds means to kill your joys with love!
Romeo and Juliet (V, iii)

This thou perceiv'st, which makes thy love more strong,
To love that well which thou must leave ere long.
Sonnet LXXIII

. . . the special thing is well obtained,
That is, her love; for that is all in all.
Taming of the Shrew (II, i)

. . . where two raging fires meet together,
They do consume the thing that feeds their fury.
Though little fire grows great with little wind,
Yet extreme gusts will blow out fire and all.
Taming of the Shrew (II, i)

Love sought is good, but given unsought, is better.
Twelfth Night (III, i)

Love is your master, for he masters you:
And he that is so yoked by a fool,
Methinks should not be chronicled for wise.
Two Gentlemen of Verona (I, i)

LOVE

Thou, Julia, thou hast metamorphos'd me;
Made me neglect my studies, lose my time,
War with good counsel, set the world at nought;
Made wit with musing weak, heart sick with thought.
             Two Gentlemen of Verona (I, i)

His little speaking shows his love but small...
They do not love, that do not show their love.
             Two Gentlemen of Verona (I, ii)

O, how this spring of love resembleth
The uncertain glory of an April day;
Which now shows all the beauty of the sun,
And by and by a cloud takes all away!
             Two Gentlemen of Verona (I, iii)

For where Love reigns, disturbing Jealousy
Doth call himself Affection's sentinel;
Gives false alarms, suggesteth mutiny,
And in a peaceful hour doth cry, 'Kill, kill;'
  Distempering gentle Love in his desire,
  As air and water do abate the fire.
             Venus and Adonis (stanza 109)

LOYALTY

Master, go on; and I will follow thee,
To the last gasp, with truth and loyalty.
                As You Like It (II, iii)

              Though those that are betray'd
Do feel the treason sharply, yet the traitor
Stands in worse case of woe...
                Cymbeline (III, iv)

No more can I be sever'd from your side,
Than can yourself yourself in twain divide.
                King Henry VI, Part I (IV, v)

That sir which serves and seeks from gain,
And follows but for form,
Will pack when it begins to rain,
And leave thee in the storm.
                King Lear (II, iv)

            ... if ever I were traitor
My name be blotted from the book of life,
And I from heaven banish'd...
                King Richard II (I, iii)

... to thee I'll faithful prove.
                Love's Labour's Lost (IV, ii)

... to thee I'll constant prove...
                Passionate Pilgrim (III)

Day serves not light more faithful than I'll be.
                Pericles (I, ii)

LOYALTY

I prithee, remember I have done thee worthy service;
Told thee no lies, made thee no mistakings, serv'd
Without grudge or grumblings.
            The Tempest (I, ii)

Men shut their doors against a setting sun.
            Timon of Athens (I, ii)

And [I] to the love and favour of my country
Commit myself, my person, and the cause.
            Titus Andronicus (I, i)

Here is my hand for my true constancy. . .
            Two Gentlemen of Verona (II, ii)

                I cannot be
Mine own, nor anything to any, if
I be not thine: to this I am most constant,
Though destiny say <u>No</u>.
            Winter's Tale (IV, iii)

LUST

O, that false fire which in his cheek so glow'd...
Would yet again betray the fore-betray'd,
And new pervert a reconciled maid!
    A Lover's Complaint (stanza 47)

Beware of them, Diana; their promises, enticements, oaths, tokens, and all these engines of lust, are not the things they go under; many a maid hath been seduced by them ... I hope I need not to advise you further; but I hope your own grace will keep you where you are, though there were no further danger known, but the modesty which is so lost.
    All's Well That Ends Well (III, v)

Alas, what danger will it be to us,
Maids as we are, to travel forth so far!
Beauty provoketh thieves sooner than gold.
    As You Like It (I, iii)

When the blood burns, how prodigal the soul...
    Hamlet (I, iii)

... and how can that be true love, which is falsely attempted?
    Love's Labour's Lost (I, ii)

But some untimely thought did instigate
His all-too-timeless speed, if none of those:
His honour, his affairs, his friends, his state,
Neglected all, with swift intent he goes
To quench the coal which in his liver glows.
O rash-false heat, wrapp'd in repentant cold...
    Lucrece (stanza 7)

LUST

For light and lust are deadly enemies...
Lucrece (stanza 97)

...Till the wicked fire of lust have melted him in his own grease.
Merry Wives of Windsor (II, i)

Look thou be true; do not give dalliance
Too much the rein: the strongest oaths are straw
To the fire i' the blood...
The Tempest (IV, i)

Lust and liberty
Creep in the minds and marrows of our youth...
Timon of Athens (IV, i)

And careless lust stirs up a desperate courage;
Planting oblivion, beating reason back,
Forgetting shame's pure blush and honour's wrack.
Venus and Adonis (stanza 93)

Call it not love, for Love to heaven is fled,
Since sweating Lust on earth usurp'd his name...
Love comforteth like sunshine after rain,
But Lust's effect is tempest after sun;
Love's gentle spring doth always fresh remain,
Lust's winter comes ere summer half be done.
Love surfeits not; Lust like a glutton dies:
Love is all truth; Lust full of forged lies.
Venus and Adonis (stanza 132-134)

... my desires
Run not before mine honour, nor my lusts
Burn hotter than my faith.
Winter's Tale (IV, iv)

MARRIAGE

His company must do his minions grace,
Whilst I at home starve for a merry look.
Hath homely age the alluring beauty took
From my poor cheek? Then he hath wasted it.
Are my discourses dull? Barren my wit? . . .
What ruins are in me that can be found,
By him not ruined? Then is he the ground
Of my defeatures. My decayed fair
A sunny look of his would soon repair.
     Comedy of Errors (II, i)

Ah, do not tear away thyself from me!
For know, my love, as easy mayst thou fall
A drop of water in the breaking gulf
And take unmingled thence that drop again,
Without addition or diminishing,
As take from me thyself, and not me too.
     Comedy of Errors (II, ii)

It is thyself, mine own self's better part,
Mine eye's clear eye, my dear heart's dearer heart,
My food, my fortune, and my sweet hope's aim,
My sole earth's Heaven, and my Heaven's claim.
     Comedy of Errors (III, ii)

*   . . . that great vow*
Which did incorporate and make us one. . .
     Julius Caesar (II, i)

God, the best maker of all marriages,
Combine your hearts in one. . .
     King Henry V (V, ii)

MARRIAGE

What priceless wealth the heavens had him lent
In the possession of his beauteous mate;
Reckoning his fortune at such high-proud rate,
That kings might be espoused to more fame,
But king nor peer to such a peerless dame.
O, happiness enjoy'd but of a few!
Lucrece (stanza 4)

Look that you love your wife, her worth worth yours.
Measure for Measure (V, i)

What's mine is yours, and what is yours is mine.
Measure for Measure (V, i)

For having such a blessing in his lady,
He finds the joys of Heaven here on earth.
And if on earth he do not mean (deserve) it, then
In reason he should never come to Heaven.
Merchant of Venice (III, v)

Pardon me, wife;—henceforth do what thou wilt...
Merry Wives of Windsor (IV, iv)

The sealing day betwixt my love and me,
For everlasting bond of fellowship—
Midsummer Night's Dream (I, i)

So smile the Heavens upon this holy act
That afterhours with sorrow chide us not!
Romeo and Juliet (II, vi)

Sir, she is mortal; but
By immortal Providence, she's mine.
The Tempest (V, i)

MERCY

O, if men were to be saved by merit, what hole in hell were hot enough for him?
  King Henry IV, Part I (I, ii)

No ceremony that to great ones 'longs. . .
Become them with one half so good a grace
As mercy does.
  Measure for Measure (II, ii)

              Oh, it is excellent
To have a giant's strength, but it is tyrannous
To use it like a giant.
  Measure for Measure (II, ii)

The quality of mercy is not strained,
It droppeth as the gentle rain from heaven
Upon the place beneath. It is twice bless'd;
It blesseth him that gives and him that takes.
'Tis mightiest in the mightiest; it becomes
The throned monarch better than his crown. . .
But mercy is above this sceptered sway. . .
It is an attribute to God himself,
And earthly power doth then show likest God's
When mercy seasons justice,
  Merchant of Venice (IV, i)

              We do pray for mercy,
And that same prayer doth teach us all to render
The deeds of mercy.
  Merchant of Venice (IV, i)

Wilt thou draw near the nature of the gods?
Draw near them, then, in being merciful:
Sweet mercy is nobility's true badge.
  Titus Andronicus (I, i)

MORALITY

>   *Such an act*
> *That blurs the grace and blush of modesty;*
> *Calls virtue hypocrite; takes off the rose*
> *From the fair forehead of an innocent love,*
> *And sets a blister there; makes marriage vows*
> *As false as dicers' oaths: O, such a deed*
> *As from the body of contraction plucks*
> *The very soul; and sweet religion makes*
> *A rhapsody of words! heaven's face doth glow...*
>   *Hamlet (III, iv)*

>   *... a villain! ...*
> *That from a shelf the precious diadem stole,*
> *And put it in his pocket!*
>   *Hamlet (III, iv)*

> *Let fair humanity abhor the deed*
> *That spots and stains love's modest snow-white weed.*
>   *Lucrece (stanza 28)*

> *Her sacred temple spotted, spoil'd, corrupted.*
>   *Lucrece (stanza 168)*

>   *Most dangerous*
> *Is that temptation that doth goad us on*
> *To sin in loving virtue.*
>   *Measure for Measure (II, ii)*

>   *... a gentlewoman of mine*
> *Who, falling in the flaws of her own youth,*
> *Hath blistered her report.*
>   *Measure for Measure (II, iii)*

MORALITY

>   . . . O, she is fallen
> Into a pit of ink! that the wide sea
> Hath drops too few to wash her clean again. . .
> > Much Ado About Nothing (IV, i)

> You're a fair viol and your sense the strings;
> Who, finger'd to make man his lawful music,
> Would draw heaven down . . . to hearken;
> But being play'd upon before your time,
> Hell only danceth at so harsh a chime. . .
> > Pericles (I, i)

> . . . my modesty, the jewel in my dower. . .
> > The Tempest (III, i)

> Then as my gift, and thine own acquisition
> Worthily purchas'd, take my daughter: but
> If thou dost break her virgin-knot before
> All sanctimonious ceremonies may
> With full and holy rite be minister'd,
> No sweet aspersion shall the heavens let fall
> To make this contract grow; but barren hate,
> Sour-ey'd disdain, and discord, shall bestrew
> The union of your bed with weeds so loathly,
> That you shall hate it both: therefore take heed. . .
> > The Tempest (IV, i)

MUSIC

. . . music oft hath such a charm
To make bad good, and good provoke to harm.
Measure for Measure (IV, i)

How sweet the moonlight sleeps upon this bank!
Here will we sit and let the sounds of music
Creep in our ears. Soft stillness and the night
Become the touches of sweet harmony.
Merchant of Venice (V, i)

. . . do but note a wild and wanton herd,
Or race of youthful and unhandled colts,
Fetching mad bounds, bellowing, and neighing loud,
Which is the hot condition of their blood.
If they but hear perchance a trumpet sound,
Or any air of music touch their ears,
You shall perceive them make a mutual stand,
Their savage eyes turned to a modest gaze
By the sweet power of music.
Merchant of Venice (V, i)

. . . naught so stockish, hard, and full of rage
But music for the time doth change his nature.
The man that hath no music in himself,
Nor is not moved with concord of sweet sounds,
Is fit for treasons, stratagems, and spoils.
The motions of his spirit are dull as night,
And his affections dark as [Hell].
Let no such man be trusted.
Merchant of Venice (V, i)

MUSIC

O good my lord, tax not so bad a voice,
To slander music any more than once.
                Much Ado About Nothing (II, iii)

       I am beholding to you,
For your sweet music this last night: I do
Protest my ears were never better fed
With such delightful pleasing harmony...
Sir, you are music's master.
                Pericles (II, v)

   . . . music was ordained!
. . . to refresh the mind of man
After his studies or his usual pain...
                Taming of the Shrew (III, i)

Where should this music be: i' th' air, or the earth?
                The Tempest (I, ii)

This music crept by me upon the waters,
Allaying both their fury and my passion
With its sweet air: thence I have follow'd it,
Or it hath drawn me rather...
                The Tempest (I, ii)

Sounds and sweet airs, that give delight, and hurt not.
                The Tempest (III, ii)

Orpheus' lute was strung with poets' sinews;
Whose golden touch could soften steel and stones,
Make tigers tame, and huge leviathans forsake
Unsounded deeps, to dance on sands
                Two Gentlemen of Verona (III, ii)

OBEDIENCE

I hourly learn a doctrine of obedience...
*   Antony and Cleopatra (V, ii)*

Ere I learn love, I'll practice to obey.
*   Comedy of Errors (II, i)*

... by his rare example ... men obeyed...
*   Coriolanus (II, ii)*

This is not well, my lord, this is not well.
What say you to it? will you again unknit
This churlish knot of all-abhorred war?
And move in that obedient orb again,
Where you did give a fair and natural light;
And be no more an exhal'd meteor,
A prodigy of fear, and a portent
Of broached mischief to the unborn times?
*   King Henry IV, Part I (V, i)*

*   Therefore doth heaven divide*
The state of man in divers functions,
Setting endeavour in continual motion;
To which is fixed, as an aim or butt,
Obedience: for so work the honey bees,
Creatures that, by a rule in nature, teach
The act of order to a peopled kingdom.
*   King Henry V (I, ii)*

We cannot but obey
The powers above us.
*   Pericles (III, iii)*

*   My commission is*
Not to reason of the deed, but do 't.
*   Pericles (IV, i)*

PARENTING

O disloyal thing,
That shouldst repair my youth, thou heap'st
A year's age on me.
   Cymbeline (I, i)

Now 'tis the spring, and woods are shallow-rooted;
Suffer them now, and they'll o'er grow the garden,
And choke the herbs for want of husbandry.
   King Henry VI, Part II (III, i)

Out on thee, rude man! thou dost shame thy mother
And wound her honour with this diffidence.
   King John (I, i)

Now, as fond fathers,
Having bound up the threatening twigs of birch
Only to stick it in their children's sight
For terror, not to use, in time the rod
Becomes more mocked than feared. . .
   Measure for Measure (I, iii)

Condemn the fault, and not the actor of it.
   Measure for Measure (II, ii)

It is a wise father that knows his own child.
   Merchant of Venice (II, ii)

Bad child, worse father! to entice his own
To evil, should be done by none.
   Pericles (induction)

Good wombs have borne bad sons.
   The Tempest (I, ii)

   [their mother. . .
. . . like unbridled children, grown too headstrong for
   Troilus and Cressida (III, ii)

PATIENCE

>   ... *a very little thief of*
> *occasion will rob you of a great deal of patience.*
>   *Coriolanus (II, i)*

> *... sit still, my soul: foul deeds will rise,*
> *Though all the earth o'erwhelm them to men's eyes!*
>   *Hamlet (I, ii)*

> *Be you content to lend your patience to us,*
> *And we shall jointly labour with your soul*
> *To give it due content.*
>   *Hamlet (IV, v)*

>   *... arming myself with patience*
> *To stay the providence of some high powers*
> *That govern us below.*
>   *Julius Caesar (V, i)*

>   *To climb steep hills*
> *Requires slow pace at first.*
>   *King Henry VIII (I, i)*

>   *We may outrun*
> *By violent swiftness that which we run at,*
> *And lose by overrunning.*
>   *King Henry VIII (I, i)*

> *Oh, reason not the need. Our basest beggars*
> *Are in the poorest thing superfluous.*
> *Allow not nature more than nature needs...*
> *You Heavens, give me that patience, patience I need!*
>   *King Lear (II, iv)*

>   *[choler...*
> *... sheathe thy impatience, throw cold water on thy*
>   *Merry Wives of Windsor (II, iii)*

__PATIENCE__

For there was never yet philosopher
That could endure the toothache patiently.
Much Ado About Nothing (V, i)

How poor are they that have not patience!
What wound did ever heal but by degrees?
Othello (II, iii)

Be patient, for the world is broad and wide.
Romeo and Juliet (III, iii)

. . . let mischance be slave to patience.
Romeo and Juliet (V, iii)

. . . bear this work of Heaven with patience.
Romeo and Juliet (V, iii)

He that will have a cake out of the wheat must needs tarry the grinding.
Troilus and Cressida (I, i)

A thousand more mischances than this one
Have learn'd me how to brook this patiently.
Two Gentlemen of Verona (V, iii)

Love, lend me patience to forbear a while.
Two Gentlemen of Verona (V, iv)

PRAYER

We, ignorant of ourselves,
Beg often our own harms, which the wise powers
Deny us for our good; so find we profit,
By losing of our prayers.
     Antony and Cleopatra (II, i)

Lovers and men in dangerous bonds pray not alike.
     Cymbeline (III, ii)

O, my offence is rank, it smells to heaven...
Pray can I not; though inclination be as sharp as will,
My stronger guilt defeats my strong intent;
And, like a man to double business bound,
I stand in pause where I shall first begin...
Bow, stubborn knees; and, heart with strings of steel,
Be soft as sinews of the new-born babe! ...
My words fly up, my thoughts remain below:
Words without thoughts never to heaven go.
     Hamlet (III, iii)

God be at your table...I pray God,—God be with you.
     Hamlet (IV, v)

A widow, husbandless, subject to fears...
A widow cries; be husband to me, heavens!
     King John (III, i)

Pray that the right may thrive.
     King Lear (V, ii)

Oh, God defend my soul from such deep sin!
     King Richard II (I, i)

Duchess: Where then, alas! may I complain myself?
Gaunt: To God, the widow's champion and defense.
     King Richard II (I, ii)

PRAYER

Pleads he in earnest? look upon his face;
His eyes do drop no tears, his prayers are in jest;
His words come from his mouth, ours from our breast.
He prays but faintly, and would be denied;
We pray with heart, and soul, and all beside.
His weary joints would gladly rise, I know;
Our knees shall kneel till to the ground they grow.
His prayers are full of false hypocrisy;
Ours of true zeal and deep integrity.
Our prayers do out-pray his; then let them have
That mercy which true prayers ought to have.
                King Richard II (V, iii)

                The Queen that bore thee,
Oftener upon her knees than on her feet...
                Macbeth (IV, iii)

When I would pray and think, I think and pray
To several subjects. Heaven hath my empty words,
Whilst my invention, hearing not my tongue,
Anchors on Isabel. Heaven in my mouth,
As if I did but only chew His name...
                Measure for Measure (II, iv)

                My ending is despair,
Unless I be reliev'd by prayer,
Which pierces so, that it assaults
Mercy itself, and frees all faults.
                The Tempest (V, i)

... for heaven shall hear our prayers...
                Titus Andronicus (III, i)

                        [pray.
Get him to say his prayers; good sir Toby, get him to
                Twelfth Night (III, iv)

PREPARATION

*Those that with haste will make a mighty fire
Begin it with weak straws.*
                Julius Caesar (I, iii)

                When we mean to build,
*We first survey the plot, then draw the model;
And when we see the figure of the house,
Then must we rate the cost of the erection;
Which if we find outweighs ability,
What do we then, but draw anew the model
In fewer offices; or, at least, desist
To build at all? . . . or else. . .
Like one, that draws the model of a house
Beyond his power to build it; who, half through,
Gives o'er, and leaves his part-created cost
A naked subject to the weeping clouds,
And waste for churlish winter's tyranny.*
                King Henry IV, Part II (I, iii)

*These should be hours for necessities,
Not for delights; times to repair our nature
With comforting repose, and not for us
To waste these times.*
                King Henry VIII (V, i)

We'll set thee to school to an ant, to teach thee there's no laboring i' the winter.
                King Lear (II, iv)

*When clouds appear, wise men put on their cloaks;
When great leaves fall, then winter is at hand;
When the sun sets, who doth not look for night?
Untimely storms make men expect a dearth. . .
Before the times of change, still is it so. . .*
                King Richard III (II, iii)

PRIDE

I am for the house with the narrow gate, which I take to be too little for pomp to enter. Some, that humble themselves, may; but the many will be too chill and tender; and they'll be for the flowery way, that leads to the broad gate, and the great fire.
All's Well That Ends Well (IV, v)

Such a nature, tickled with good success,
Disdains the shadow which he treads on at noon.
Coriolanus (I, i)

. . . pride . . . ever taints the happy man. . .
Coriolanus (IV, vii)

Costly thy habit as thy purse can buy,
But not express'd in fancy; rich, not gaudy:
For the apparel oft proclaims the man. . .
Hamlet (I, iii)

Conceit in weakest bodies strongest works. . .
Hamlet (III, iv)

Your wisdom is consumed in confidence.
Julius Caesar (II, ii)

Small things make base men proud. . .
King Henry VI, Part II (IV, i)

I have ventured,
Like little wanton boys that swim on bladders, . . .
Far beyond my depth.
King Henry VIII (III, ii)

For there was never yet fair woman but she made mouths in a glass.
King Lear (III, ii)

PRIDE

Would he not stumble? Would he not fall down,
(Since pride must have a fall,) and break the neck
Of that proud man...
           King Richard II (V, v)

They that stand high have mighty blasts to shake them;
And if they fall, they dash themselves to pieces.
           King Richard III (I, iii)

                  But man, proud man,
Dressed in a little brief authority,
Most ignorant of what he's most assured,
His glassy essence...
Plays such fantastic tricks before high Heaven
As make the angels weep...
           Measure for Measure (II, ii)

The worthiness of praise disdains his worth,
If that the praised himself bring the praise forth.
           Troilus and Cressida (I, ii)

                                      [glass,
He that is proud eats up himself; pride is his own
His own trumpet, his own chronicle;
And whatever praises itself but in the deed,
Devours the deed in the praise.
           Troilus and Cressida (II, i)

        ... pride hath no other glass
To show itself but pride; for supple knees
Feed arrogance, and are the proud man's fees.
           Troilus and Cressida (III, iii)

... how apt the poor are to be proud!
           Twelfth Night (III, i)

RECORD KEEPING

. . . good phrases are surely, and ever were, very commendable.
King Henry IV, Part II (III, ii)

. . . let this be copied out,
And keep it safe for our remembrance:
Return the precedent to these lords again,
That, having our fair order written down,
Both they, and we, perusing o'er these notes,
May know wherefore we took the sacrament,
And keep our faiths firm and inviolable.
King John (V, ii)

I will set down what comes . . . to satisfy my remembrance the more strongly.
Macbeth (V, i)

Your name from hence immortal life shall have,
Though I, once gone, to all the world must die:
The earth can yield me but a common grave,
When you entombed in men's eyes shall lie.
Your monument shall be my gentle verse,
Which eyes not yet created shall o'er-read;
And tongues to be your being shall rehearse,
When all the breathers of this world are dead;
You still shall live,—such virtue hath my pen. . .
Sonnet LXXXI

. . . in black ink my love may still shine bright.
Sonnet LXV

I pray you let us satisfy our eyes
With the memorials and the things of fame,
That do renown this city.
Twelfth Night (III, iii)

REPENTANCE

No evil lost is wailed when it is gone.
          Comedy of Errors (IV, ii)

What custom wills, in all things should we do 't,
The dust on antique time would lie unswept,
And mountainous error be too highly heaped
For truth to o'erpeer.
          Coriolanus (II, iii)

          If you will pass
To where you are bound, you must inquire your way,
Which you are out of, with a gentler spirit. . .
          Coriolanus (III, i)

There is differency between a grub and a butterfly, yet your butterfly was a grub.
          Coriolanus (V, iv)

          I have heard
That guilty creatures, sitting at a play,
Have by the very cunning of the scene
Been struck so to the soul, that presently
They have proclaim'd their malefactions. . .
          Hamlet (II, ii)

May one be pardon'd, and retain the offence?
          Hamlet (III, iii)

          Confess yourself to heaven;
Repent what's past; avoid what is to come;
And do not spread the compost on the weeds,
To make them ranker.
          Hamlet (III, iv)

REPENTANCE

So every bondman in his own hand bears
The power to cancel his captivity.
                Julius Caesar (I, iii)

... to wish
Things done undone.
                Julius Caesar (IV, ii)

Well, I'll repent, and that suddenly, while I am in
some liking; I shall be out of heart shortly, and then
I shall have no strength to repent. An I have not
forgotten what the inside of a church is made of...
                King Henry IV, Part I (III, iii)

For God doth know, so shall the world perceive,
That I have turn'd away my former self...
                King Henry IV, Part II (V, v)

I know myself now, and I feel within me
A peace above all earthly dignities,
A still and quiet conscience.
                King Henry VIII (III, ii)

... evils, that take leave,
On their departure most of all shew evil...
                King John (III, iv)

The breath of heaven hath blown his spirit out,
And strew'd repentant ashes on his head.
                King John (IV, i)

Unthread the rude eye of rebellion,
And welcome home again discarded faith.
                King John (V, iv)

REPENTANCE

Woe, that too late repents.
King Lear (I, iv)

But, ere I last receiv'd the sacrament,
I did confess it; and exactly begg'd
Your grace's pardon...
King Richard II (I, i)

Since thou hast far to go, bear not along
The clogging burthen of a guilty soul.
King Richard II (I, iii)

I charge you, as you hope to have redemption
By Christ's dear blood shed for our grievous sins...
King Richard II (I, iv)

Fear, and not love, begets his penitence:
Forget to pity him lest thy pity prove
A serpent that will sting thee to the heart.
King Richard II (V, iii)

Come, my old son;—I pray God make thee new.
King Richard II (V, iii)

Unnatural deeds
Do breed unnatural troubles. Infected minds
To their deaf pillows will discharge their secrets.
More needs she the divine than the physician.
Macbeth (V, i)

Mac: Cleanse the stuffed bosom of that perilous stuff
Which weighs upon the heart.
Doc: Therein the patient
Must minister to himself.
Macbeth (V, iii)

REPENTANCE

. . . happy are they that hear their detractions, and can put them to mending.
Much Ado About Nothing (II, iii)

Were I chief lord of all this spacious world,
I'd give it to undo the deed.
Pericles (IV, iii)

. . . I have learned me to repent the sin
Of disobedient opposition. . .
Romeo and Juliet (IV, ii)

My heart is wondrous light
Since this same wayward girl is so reclaimed.
Romeo and Juliet (IV, ii)

What though her frowning brows be bent,
Her cloudy looks will clear ere night;
And then too late she will repent. . .
Passionate Pilgrim (XVII)

Unheedful vows may heedfully be broken;
And he wants wit that wants resolved will
To learn his wit to exchange the bad for better.
Two Gentlemen of Verona (II, vi)

My shame and guilt confounds me...if hearty sorrow
Be a sufficient ransom for offence, I tender't here;
I do as truly suffer as err I did commit. . .
Who by repentance is not satisfied
Is nor of heaven, nor earth; for these are pleased;
By penitence the Eternal's wrath's appeas'd.
Two Gentlemen of Verona (V, iv)

REPUTATION

. . . his clothes made a false report of him.
Coriolanus (IV, v)

Let me make men know
More valour in me than my habits (clothes) show.
Cymbeline (V, i)

The evil that men do lives after them,
The good is oft interred with their bones.
Julius Caesar (III, ii)

And when old Time shall lead him to his end,
Goodness and he fill up one monument!
King Henry VIII (II, i)

The purest treasure mortal times afford
Is—spotless reputation; that away,
Men are but gilded loam, or painted clay. . .
Mine honour is my life; both grow in one;
Take honour from me, and my life is done. . .
King Richard II (I, i)

Opinion's but a fool, that makes us scan
The outward habit by the inward man.
Pericles (II, ii)

Thence comes it that my name receives a brand. . .
Which vulgar scandal stamp'd upon my brow;
Sonnets CXI, CXII

He lives in fame that died in virtue's cause.
Titus Andronicus (I, i)

SELF-CONTROL

> *His heart's his mouth—*
> *What his breast forges, that his tongue must vent...*
> *Coriolanus (III, i)*

> *— Give me that man*
> *That is not passion's slave, and I will wear him*
> *In my heart's core, ay, in my heart of heart,*
> *As I do thee.*
> *Hamlet (III, ii)*

> *This strained passion doth you wrong, my lord...*
> *The lives of all your loving complices*
> *Lean on your health; the which, if you give o'er*
> *To stormy passion, must perforce decay.*
> *King Henry IV, Part II (I, i)*

> *Most subject is the fattest soil to weeds,*
> *And he, the noble image of my youth,*
> *Is over-spread with them; therefore my grief*
> *Stretches itself beyond the hour of death.*
> *The blood weeps from my heart, when I do shape,*
> *In forms imaginary, the unguided days,*
> *And rotten times, that you shall look upon*
> *When I am sleeping with my ancestors.*
> *For when his headstrong riot hath no curb,*
> *When rage and hot blood are his counsellors,*
> *When means and lavish manners meet together,*
> *O, with what wings shall his affections fly*
> *Towards fronting peril and oppos'd decay!*
> *King Henry IV, Part II (IV, iv)*

> *... she was a queen*
> *Over her passion, who most rebel-like*
> *Sought to be king o'er her.*
> *King Lear (IV, iii)*

SELF-CONTROL

Methinks I am a prophet new inspir'd,
And thus, expiring, do foretell of him:
His rash fierce blaze of riot cannot last,
For violent fires soon burn out themselves;
Small showers last long, but sudden storms are short;
He tires betimes, that spurs too fast betimes;
With eager feeding, food doth choke the feeder:
Light vanity, insatiate cormorant,
Consuming means, soon preys upon itself.
    King Richard II (II, i)

Therefore, brave conquerors!—for so you are,
That war against your own affections,
And the huge army of the world's desires. . .
    Love's Labour's Lost (I, i)

    . . . one who never feels
The wanton stings and motions of the sense,
But doth rebate and blunt his natural edge
With profits of the mind, study and fast.
    Measure for Measure (I, iv)

    Boundless intemperance
In nature is a tyranny. It hath been
The untimely emptying of the happy throne,
And fall of many kings.
    Macbeth (IV, iii)

. . . but we have reason to cool our raging motions,
our carnal stings, our unbitted lusts. . .
    Othello (I, iii)

They that have power to hurt and will do none. . .
And are to temptation slow;
They rightly do inherit heaven's graces. . .
    Sonnet XCIV

SELFISHNESS

Shall we serve Heaven
With less respect than we do minister
To our gross selves?
Measure for Measure (II, ii)

. . . being overfull of self-affairs. . .
Midsummer Night's Dream (I, i)

. . . she cannot love,
Nor take no shape nor project of affection,
She is so self-endeared.
Much Ado About Nothing (III, i)

Princes . . . should live like gods above,
Who freely give to every one that comes to honour
them.
Pericles (II, iii)

For having traffic with thyself alone,
Thou of thyself thy sweet self dost deceive.
Sonnet IV

To grow unto himself was his desire. . .
Venus and Adonis (stanza 197)

SERVICE

. . . find the way to heaven
By doing deeds of hospitality. . .
As You Like It (II, iv)

. . . words are but wind. . .
Comedy of Errors (III, i)

. . . rewards
His deeds with doing them, and is content
To spend the time. . .
Coriolanus (II, ii)

They know the corn
Was not our recompense, resting well assured
They ne'er did service for 't.
Coriolanus (III, i)

So service shall with steeled sinew toil,
And labour shall refresh itself with hope. . .
King Henry V (II, ii)

. . . no day without a deed to crown it.
King Henry VIII (V, v)

The service and the loyalty I owe . . . pays itself.
Macbeth (I, iv)

I have no superfluous leisure. My stay must be stolen
out of other affairs, but I will attend you awhile.
Measure for Measure (III, i)

I never did repent for doing good,
Nor shall not now.
Merchant of Venice (III, iv)

SERVICE

He is well paid that is well satisfied.
Merchant of Venice (IV, i)

How far that little candle throws his beams!
So shines a good deed in a naughty world.
Merchant of Venice (V, i)

Masters, do you serve God?
Much Ado About Nothing (IV, ii)

. . . the more I give to thee,
The more I have, for both are infinite.
Romeo and Juliet (II, ii)

'Tis deeds must win the prize. . .
Taming of the Shrew (II, i)

'Tis not enough to help the feeble up,
But to support him after.
Timon of Athens (I, i)

We are born to do benefits. . .
Timon of Athens (I, ii)

SIN

> . . . *he must have a long spoon*
> *That must eat with the Devil.*
> *Comedy of Errors (IV, iii)*

> *O error, soon conceived,*
> *Thou never comest unto a happy birth...*
> *Julius Caesar (V, iii)*

> *These things, indeed, you have articulated,*
> *Proclaim'd at market-crosses, read in churches,*
> *To face the garment of rebellion*
> *With some fine colour, that may please the eye...*
> *King Henry IV, Part I (V, i)*

> *Now neighbour confines, purge you of your scum!*
> *Have you a ruffian, that will swear, drink, dance,*
> *Revel the night; rob, murder, and commit*
> *The oldest sins the newest kind of ways?*
> *King Henry IV, Part II (IV, iv)*

> *I will weep for thee;*
> *For this revolt of thine, methinks, is like*
> *Another fall of man.*
> *King Henry V (II, ii)*

> *Though you, and all the kings of Christendom,*
> *Are led so grossly by this meddling priest,*
> *Dreading the curse that money may buy out;*
> *And by the merit of vile gold, dross, dust,*
> *Purchase corrupted pardon of a man,*
> *Who, in that sale, sells pardon from himself;*
> *Though you, and all the rest, so grossly led,*
> *This juggling witchcraft with revenue cherish;*
> *Yet I alone, alone do me oppose*
> *Against the pope, and count his friends my foes.*
> *King John (III, i)*

SIN

And oftentimes excusing of a fault
Doth make the fault the worse by the excuse;
As patches, set upon a little breach
Discredit more in hiding of the fault,
Than did the fault before it was so patch'd.
   King John (IV, ii)

Wisdom and goodness to the vile seem vile.
Filths savor but themselves.
   King Lear (IV, ii)

. . . our pleasant vices
Make instruments to plague us.
   King Lear (V, iii)

To find out right with wrong, it may not be;
And you that do abet him in this kind,
Cherish rebellion, and are rebels all.
   King Richard II (II, iii)

O, forbid it, God,
That, in a Christian climate, souls refin'd
Should show so heinous, black, obscene a deed!
   King Richard II (IV, i)

That through the length of time he stands disgrac'd:
Besides, his soul's fair temple is defac'd. . .
   Lucrece (stanza 103)

But no perfection is so absolute,
That some impurity doth not pollute. . .
Unwholesome weeds take root with precious flowers;
What virtue breeds iniquity devours. . .
   Lucrece (stanzas 122, 125)

<u>SIN</u>

[man...
... mine eternal jewel given to the common enemy of
Macbeth (III, i)

By the pricking of my thumbs,
Something wicked this way comes.
Macbeth (IV, i)

O my dread lord,
I should be guiltier than my guiltiness
To think I can be undiscernible.
Measure for Measure (V, i)

There is no vice so simple but assumes
Some mark of virtue on his outward parts.
Merchant of Venice (III, ii)

Few love to hear the sins they love to act...
Pericles (I, i)

One sin, I know, another doth provoke;
Murder's as near to lust as flame to smoke:
Poison and treason are the hands of sin...
Pericles (I, i)

Give me my sin again.
Romeo and Juliet (I, v)

... violent delights have violent ends...
Romeo and Juliet (II, vi)

For sweetest things turn sourest by their deeds;
Lilies that fester smell far worse than weeds.
Sonnet XCIV

... I ... sold cheap what is most dear...
Sonnet CX

SIN

Still losing when I saw myself to win!
What wretched errors hath my heart committed...
    Sonnet CXIX

Sometimes we are devils to ourselves, when we will tempt the frailty of our powers, presuming on their changeful potency.
            Troilus and Cressida (IV, i)

Dost thou think because thou art virtuous, there shall be no more cakes and ale?
            Twelfth Night (II, iii)

SORROW

Jaq: Why, 'tis good to be sad and say nothing.
Ros: Why then, 'tis good to be a post.
As You Like It (IV, i)

When sorrows come, they come not single spies,
But in battalias!
Hamlet (IV, v)

Passion, I see, is catching, for mine eyes,
Seeing those beads of sorrow stand in thine,
Began to water.
Julius Caesar (III, i)

For grief is proud,
And makes his owner stout . . . my grief's so great
That no supporter but the huge firm earth
Can hold it up: here I and sorrows sit;
Here is my throne, bid kings come bow to it.
King John (III, i)

For sorrow ends not when it seemeth done.
King Richard II (I, ii)

Joy absent, grief is present for that time. . .
But grief makes one hour ten.
King Richard II (I, iii)

Look, what thy soul holds dear, imagine it
To lie that way thou go'st, not whence thou com'st.
Suppose the singing birds, musicians;
The grass whereon thou tread'st, the presence strew'd;
The flowers, fair ladies; and thy steps, no more
Than a delightful measure, or a dance:
For gnarling sorrow hath less power to bite
The man that mocks at it, and sets it light.
King Richard II (I, iii)

SORROW

Each substance of a grief hath twenty shadows,
Which shows like grief itself, but is not so:
For sorrow's eye, glazed with blinding tears,
Divides, one thing entire, to many objects. . .
    King Richard II (II, ii)

Sorrow breaks seasons and reposing hours,
Makes the night morning, and the noon-tide night.
    King Richard III (I, iv)

Mirth cannot move a soul in agony.
    Love's Labour's Lost (V, ii)

And fellowship in woe doth woe assuage. . .
    Lucrece (stanza 113)

Sad souls are slain in merry company;
Grief best is pleas'd with grief's society:
True sorrow then is feelingly suffic'd
When with like semblance it is sympathiz'd.
    Lucrece (stanza 159)

For sorrow, like a heavy-hanging bell,
Once set on ringing, with his own weight goes;
Then little strength rings out the doleful knell. . .
    Lucrece (stanza 214)

Short time seems long in sorrow's sharp sustaining:
Though woe be heavy, yet it seldom sleeps;
And they that watch see time how slow it creeps.
    Lucrece (stanza 225)

Let us seek out some desolate shade, and there
Weep our sad bosoms empty.
    Macbeth (IV, iii)

SORROW

Give sorrow words. The grief that does not speak
Whispers the o'erfraught heart, and bids it break.
Macbeth (IV, iii)

The night is long that never finds the day.
Macbeth (IV, iii)

Why is your cheek so pale?
How chance the roses there do fade so fast?
Midsummer Night's Dream (I, i)

So sorrow's heaviness doth heavier grow
For debt that bankrupt sleep doth sorrow owe. . .
Midsummer Night's Dream (III, ii)

Well, every one can master a grief, but he that has it.
Much Ado About Nothing (III, ii)

Charm ache with air, and agony with words?
No, no; 'tis all men's office to speak patience
To those that wring under the load of sorrow;
But no man's virtue nor sufficiency,
To be so moral, when he shall endure
The like himself. . .
Much Ado About Nothing (V, i)

. . . Shall we rest us here,
And by relating tales of others' griefs,
See if 'twill teach us to forget our own?
Pericles (II, iv)

He that is stricken blind cannot forget
The precious treasure of his eyesight lost.
Romeo and Juliet (I, i)

SORROW

Good night, good night! Parting is such sweet sorrow
That I shall say good night till it be morrow.
          Romeo and Juliet (II, ii)

Some grief shows much of love,
But much of grief shows still some want of wit.
          Romeo and Juliet (III, v)

Is there no pity sitting in the clouds
That sees into the bottom of my grief?
          Romeo and Juliet (III, v)

And yet, love knows, it is a greater grief
To bear love's wrong, than hate's known injury.
          Sonnet XL

Do not draw back, for we will mourn with thee:
O, could our mourning ease thy misery.
          Titus Andronicus (II, iv)

Sorrow concealed, like an oven stopp'd,
Doth burn the heart to cinders where it is.
          Titus Andronicus (II, v)

Is not my sorrow deep, having no bottom? . . .
When heaven doth weep, doth not the earth o'erflow?
These miseries are more than may be borne.
To weep with them that weep doth ease some deal;
But sorrow flouted at is double death.
          Titus Andronicus (III, i)

For misery is trodden on by many,
And being low never reliev'd by any.
          Venus and Adonis (stanza 118)

TEMPTATION

> . . . *lest myself be guilty to self-wrong,*
> *I'll stop mine ears against the mermaid's song.*
> *Comedy of Errors (III, ii)*

> *Therefore it is meet*
> *That noble minds keep ever with their likes,*
> *For who so firm that cannot be seduced?*
> *Julius Caesar (I, ii)*

> *. . . by night,*
> *When evils are most free. . .*
> *Julius Caesar (II, i)*

> *The storm is up, and all is on the hazard.*
> *Julius Caesar (V, i)*

> *I fear me, you but warm the starved snake,*
> *Who, cherish'd in your breasts, will sting your hearts.*
> *King Henry VI, Part II (III, i)*

> *And many strokes, though with a little axe,*
> *Hew down and fell the hardest-timber'd oak.*
> *King Henry VI, Part III (II, i)*

> *. . . stand fast; the devil tempts thee here,*
> *In likeness of a new uptrimmed bride.*
> *King John (III, i)*

> *. . . so it is sometimes,*
> *Glory grows guilty of detested crimes;*
> *When, for fame's sake, for praise, an outward part,*
> *We bend. . .*
> *Love's Labour's Lost (IV, i)*

> *Devils soonest tempt, resembling spirits of light.*
> *Love's Labour's Lost (IV, iii)*

TEMPTATION

For by our ears our hearts oft tainted be...
               Lucrece (stanza 6)

And die, unhallow'd thoughts, before you blot
With your uncleanness that which is divine!
               Lucrece (stanza 28)

What win I, if I gain the thing I seek?
A dream, a breath, a froth of fleeting joy.
Who buys a minute's mirth to wail a week?
Or sells eternity to get a toy?
For one sweet grape who will the vine destroy?
               Lucrece (stanza 31)

I have debated, even in my soul,
What wrong, what shame, what sorrow I shall breed...
I know repentant tears ensue the deed,
Reproach, disdain, and deadly enmity;
Yet strive I to embrace mine infamy.
               Lucrece (stanza 72)

'Tis one thing to be tempted...
Another thing to fall.
               Measure for Measure (II, i)

O cunning enemy, that to catch a saint
With saints dost bait thy hook!
               Measure for Measure (II, ii)

He's no man on whom perfections wait
That, knowing sin within, will touch the gate.
               Pericles (I, i)

        O mischief, thou art swift
To enter in the thoughts of desperate men!
               Romeo and Juliet (V, i)

TIME

Let's take the instant by the forward top,
For we are old, and on our quick'st decrees
The inaudible and noiseless foot of time
Steals, ere we can effect them.
All's Well That Ends Well (V, iii)

. . . Time comes stealing on by night and day. . .
Comedy of Errors (IV, ii)

Our hands are full of business, let's away;
Advantage feeds him fat, while men delay.
King Henry IV, Part I (III, ii)

Well, thus we play the fools with the time; and the
spirits of the wise sit in the clouds, and mock us.
King Henry IV, Part II (II, ii)

I wasted time, and now doth time waste me. . .
King Richard II (V, v)

Let every man be master of his time. . .
Macbeth (III, i)

We burn daylight.
Merry Wives of Windsor (II, i) &
Romeo and Juliet (I, iv)

...better three hours too soon than a minute too late.
Merry Wives of Windsor (II, ii)

. . . hasty-footed time. . .
Midsummer Night's Dream (III, ii)

Come, gentlemen, we sit too long on trifles,
And waste the time. . .
Pericles (II, iii)

TIME

. . . Time's the king of men
For he's their parent, and he is their grave,
And gives them what he will, not what they crave.
Pericles (II, iv)

. . . in delay
We waste our lights in vain, like lamps by day.
Romeo and Juliet (I, iv)

The hour's now come;
The very minute bids thee ope thine ear;
Obey, and be attentive. . .
The Tempest (I, ii)

For time is like a fashionable host,
That slightly shakes his parting guest by the hand;
And with his arms outstretch'd, as he would fly,
Grasps-in the comer: the welcome ever smiles,
And farewell goes out sighing.
Troilus and Cressida (III, iii)

I have important business, the tide whereof is now.
Troilus and Cressida (V, i)

The clock upbraids me with the waste of time.
Twelfth Night (III, i)

Make use of time, let not advantage slip;
Venus and Adonis (stanza 22)

TOLERANCE

He hath disgraced me . . . scorned my nation . . . heated mine enemies. And what's his reason? I am a Jew. Hath not a Jew eyes? Hath not a Jew hands, organs, dimensions, sense, affections, passions? Fed with the same food, hurt with the same weapons, subject to the same diseases, healed by the same means, warmed and cooled by the same winter and summer as a Christian is? If you prick us, do we not bleed? If you tickle us, do we not laugh? If you poison us, do we not die? And if you wrong us, shall we not revenge? If we are like you in the rest, we will resemble you in that.

Merchant of Venice (III, i)

TRUST

I will never trust a man again, for keeping his sword clean; nor believe he can have every thing in him, by wearing his apparel neatly.
All's Well That Ends Well (IV, iii)

Duke: . . . I trust thee not.
Rosa: Yet your mistrust cannot make me a traitor...
As You Like It (I, iii)

For treason is but trusted like the fox;
Who, ne'er so tame, so cherish'd, and lock'd up,
Will have a wild trick of his ancestors.
King Henry IV, Part I (V, ii)

The bird, that hath been limed in a bush,
With trembling wings disdoubteth every bush. . .
King Henry VI, Part III (V, vi)

I trust I may not trust thee; for thy word
Is but the vain breath of a common man:
Believe me, I do not believe thee, man. . .
King John (III, i)

Alb: Well, you may fear too far.
Gon: Safer than trust too far.
King Lear (I, iv)

Pawning his honour to obtain his lust;
And for himself, himself he must forsake:
Then where is truth, if there be no self-trust?
When shall he think to find a stranger just,
  When he himself, himself confounds, betrays
  To slanderous tongues and wretched hateful days?
Lucrece (stanza 23)

TRUTH

And I can teach thee . . . to shame the devil,
By telling truth. <u>Tell truth, and shame the devil</u>. . .
O, while you live, <u>tell truth, and shame the devil</u>.
    King Henry IV, Part I (III, i)

Truth loves open dealing.
    King Henry VIII (III, i)

Ye speak like honest men; pray God, ye prove so!
    King Henry VIII (III, i)

*   . . . and delight*
No less in truth than life.
    Macbeth (IV, iii)

. . . it is ten times true, for truth is truth
To the end of reckoning.
    Measure for Measure (V, i)

Truth will come to light. . .
    Merchant of Venice (II, ii)

It is not enough to speak, but to speak true.
    Midsummer Night's Dream (V, i)

For oft the eye mistakes, the brain being troubled.
    Venus and Adonis (stanza 178)

VALUE

What is the city but the people?
  Coriolanus (III, i)

The jewel that we find, we stoop and take't,
Because we see it, but what we do not see
We tread upon, and never think of it.
  Measure for Measure (II, i)

His reasons are as two grains of wheat hid in two bushels of chaff. You shall seek all day ere you find them, and when you have them, they are not worth the search.
  Merchant of Venice (I, i)

Who riseth from a feast
With that keen appetite that he sits down? . . .
  All things that are,
Are with more spirit chased than enjoyed.
  Merchant of Venice (II, vi)

The weakest kind of fruit drops earliest to the ground.
  Merchant of Venice (IV, i)

The crow doth sing as sweetly as the lark
When neither is attended. . .
How many things by season seasoned are
To their right praise and true perfection!
  Merchant of Venice (V, i)

What's in a name? That which we call a rose
By any other name would smell as sweet.
  Romeo and Juliet (II, ii)

For naught so vile that on the earth doth live,
But to the earth some special good doth give.
  Romeo and Juliet (II, iii)

VIRTUE

My chastity's the jewel of our house,
Bequeathed down from many ancestors;
Which were the greatest obloquy i' the world,
In me to lose.
                      All's Well That Ends Well (IV, ii)

. . . the people praise her for her virtues. . .
                      As You Like It (I, ii)

Perhaps he loves you now;
And now no soil nor cautel doth besmirch
The virtue of his will; but you must fear. . .
Then weigh what loss your honour may sustain,
If with too credent ear you list his songs;
Or lose your heart; or your chaste treasure open
To his unmaster'd importunity.
Fear it, Ophelia, fear it, my dear sister;
And keep you in the rear of your affection,
Out of the shot and danger of desire.
The chariest maid is prodigal enough,
If she unmask her beauty to the moon. . .
Be wary, then; best safety lies in fear:
Youth to itself rebels, though none else near.
                      Hamlet (I, iii)

But virtue, as it never will be mov'd,
Though lewdness court it in a shape of heaven. . .
                      Hamlet (I, v)

. . . be thou as chaste as ice, as pure as snow. . .
                      Hamlet (III, i)

My heart laments that virtue cannot live
Out of the teeth of emulation.
                      Julius Caesar (II, ii)

VIRTUE

'Tis beauty that doth oft make women proud...
'Tis virtue that doth make them most admir'd...
King Henry VI, Part III (I, iv)

... tell me, didst thou never hear
That things ill got had ever bad success?
And happy always was it for that son,
Whose father for his hoarding went to hell?
I'll leave my son my virtuous deeds behind;
And would my father had left me no more!
King Henry VI, Part III (II, ii)

Thyself and thy belongings
Are not thine own so proper as to waste
Thyself upon thy virtues, they on thee.
Heaven doth with us as we with torches do,
Not light them for themselves; for if our virtues
Did not go forth of us, 'twere all alike
As if we had them not.
Measure for Measure (I, i)

The hand that hath made you fair hath made you good. The goodness that is cheap in beauty makes beauty brief in goodness, but grace, being the soul of your complexion, shall keep the body of it ever fair.
Measure for Measure (III, i)

Virtue is bold, and goodness never fearful.
Measure for Measure (III, i)

... there is sense in truth and truth in virtue...
Measure for Measure (V, i)

VIRTUE

Thou art a piece of virtue, and
I doubt not but thy training hath been noble.
Pericles (IV, vi)

Virtue preserved from fell destruction's blast,
Led on by heaven and crown'd with joy at last.
Pericles (V, iii)

Virtue itself turns vice, being misapplied. . .
Romeo and Juliet (II, iii)

Kindness in women, not their beauteous looks,
Shall win my love;
Taming of the Shrew (IV, ii)

. . . look you,
A sweet virtue in a maid with clean hands.
Two Gentlemen of Verona (III, i)

WAR

Our legions are brimful, our cause is ripe.
The enemy increaseth every day...
            Julius Caesar (IV, iii)

In peace, there's nothing so becomes a man,
As modest stillness and humility;
But when the blast of war blows in our ears,
Then imitate the action of the tiger;
Stiffen the sinews, summon up the blood,
Disguise fair nature with hard-favour'd rage;
Then lend the eye a terrible aspect...
Now set the teeth, and stretch the nostril wide;
Hold hard the breath, and bend up every spirit
To his full height!—On, on, you noble English,
Whose blood is fet from fathers of war-proof!—
Fathers that, like so many Alexanders,
Have in these parts from morn till even fought,
And sheath'd their swords for lack of argument:—
Dishonour not your mothers; now attest,
That those, whom you call'd fathers, did beget you!
Be copy now to men of grosser blood,
And teach them how to war!
            King Henry V (III, i)

But if the cause be not good, the king himself hath a heavy reckoning to make, when all those legs, and arms, and heads, chopped off in a battle, shall join together at the latter day, and cry all—We died at such a place...

            King Henry V (IV, i)

WAR

The Battle of Agincourt

Exe: There's Five to one; besides, they all are fresh...

Sal: God's arm strike with us! 'tis a fearful odds.
    God buy you, princes all; I'll to my charge:
    If we no more meet, till we meet in heaven...

King: We few, we happy few, we band of brothers;
    For he to-day that sheds his blood with me,
    Shall be my brother; be he ne'er so vile,
    This day shall gentle his condition:
    And gentlemen in England, now a-bed, [here;
    Shall think themselves accurs'd, they were not
    And hold their manhoods cheap, whiles any
        speaks,
    That fought with us upon saint Crispin's day...
    Praised be God, and not our strength for it!...
              O God, thy arm was here,
    And not to us, but to thy arm alone,
    Ascribe we all!...
    And be it death proclaimed through our host,
    To boast of this, or take that praise from God,
    Which is his only.

Win: He was a king bless'd of the King of kings.
    Unto the French the dreadful judgment-day
    So dreadful will not be, as was his sight.
    The battles of the Lord of hosts he fought:
    The church's prayers made him so prosperous.

                King Henry V (IV, iii, vii, viii) &
                King Henry VI, Part I (I, i)

WAR

To whom do lions cast their gentle look?
Not to the beast that would usurp their den...
The smallest worm will turn, being trodden on;
And doves will peck in safeguard of their brood...
Unreasonable creatures feed their young;
And though man's face be fearful to their eyes,
Yet, in protection of their tender ones...
Make war with him that climb'd unto their nest,
Off'ring their own lives in their young's defence?
                      King Henry VI, Part III (II, ii)

O piteous spectacle! O bloody times!
Whiles lions war and battle for their dens,
Poor harmless lambs abide their enmity.—
Weep, wretched man...
                King Henry VI, Part III (II, v)

We must awake endeavour for defence,
For courage mounteth with occasion...
                King John (II, i)

And France, whose armour conscience buckled on,
Whom zeal and charity brought to the field
As God's own soldier...
              King John (II, ii)

For he that steeps his safety in true blood
Shall find but bloody safety, and untrue.—
              King John (III, iv)

        ... I pray you, bear me hence
From forth the noise and rumour of the field
Where I may think the remnant of my thoughts
In peace, and part this body and my soul
With contemplation and devout desires.
              King John (V, iv)

WAR

O Thou, whose captain I account myself,
Look on my forces with a gracious eye!
Put in their hands thy bruising irons of wrath,
That they may crush down with a heavy fall
The usurping helmets of our adversaries!
Make us thy ministers of chastisement,
That we may praise thee in thy victory!
To thee I do commend my watchful soul,
Ere I let fall the windows of mine eyes;
Sleeping, and waking, O, defend me still! . . .

God and our good cause fight upon our side;
The prayers of holy saints and wronged souls,
Like high-rear'd bulwarks, stand before our faces. . .
Then, if you fight against God's enemy,
God will, in justice, ward you as his soldiers;
If you do sweat to put a tyrant down,
You sleep in peace, the tyrant being slain. . .
If you do fight in safeguard of your wives,
Your wives shall welcome home the conquerors;
If you do free your children from the sword,
Your children's children quit it in your age.
Then, in the name of God, and all these rights,
Advance your standards, draw your willing swords...
Sound, drums and trumpets, bold and cheerfully'
God, and Saint George! Richmond, and victory!
King Richard III (V, iii)

WEALTH

My crown is in my heart, not on my head;
Not deck'd with diamond, and Indian stones,
Nor to be seen. My crown is call'd content,—
A crown it is that seldom kings enjoy.
King Henry VI, Part III (III, i)

Our content is our best having.
King Henry VIII (II, iii)

God in thy good cause make thee prosperous!
King Richard II (I, iii)

So then he hath it, when he cannot use it,
And leaves it to be master'd by his young,
Who in their pride do presently abuse it:
Their father was too weak, and they too strong,
To hold their cursed-blessed fortune long.
  The sweets we wish for turn to loathed sours,
  Even in the moment that we call them ours.
Lucrece (stanza 124)

If thou art rich, thou'rt poor,
For, like an ass whose back with ingots bows,
Thou bear'st thy heavy riches but a journey,
And death unloads thee.
Measure for Measure (III, i)

All that glisters is not gold,
Often have you heard that told.
Many a man his life hath sold
But my outside to behold.
Merchant of Venice (II, vii)

Who would not wish to be from wealth exempt,
Since riches point to misery and contempt?
Timon of Athens (IV, ii)

WISDOM

The fool doth think he is wise, but the wise man knows himself to be a fool.
  As You Like It (V, i)

... what he hath scanted men in hair, he hath given them in wit ... but there's many a man hath more hair than wit.
  Comedy of Errors (II, ii)

Good reasons must of force give place to better.
  Julius Caesar (IV, iii)

... for wisdom cries out in the streets, and no man regards it.
  King Henry IV, Part I (I, ii)

The better part of valour is, discretion...
  King Henry IV, Part I (V, iv)

... divorce not wisdom from your honour.
  King Henry IV, Part II (I, i)

Do what you will; your wisdom be your guide.
  King Henry IV, Part II (II, iii)

As you are old and reverend, you should be wise.
  King Lear (I, iv)

                                        [wise.
Thou shouldst not have been old till thou hadst been
  King Lear (I, v)

WISDOM

*He hath a wisdom that doth guide his valor
To act in safety.*
> *Macbeth (III, i)*

The will of man is by his reason swayed...
> *Midsummer Night's Dream (II, ii)*

> *... then must you speak
Of one, that lov'd not wisely, but too well...*
>> *Othello (V, ii)*

*He was a wise fellow and had good discretion that,
being bid to ask what he would of the king, desired
he might know none of his secrets.*
> *Pericles (I, iii)*

Wisely and slow. They stumble that run fast.
> *Romeo and Juliet (II, iii)*

'Tis age that nourisheth.
> *Taming of the Shrew (II, i)*

Let thy fair wisdom, not thy passion sway...
> *Twelfth Night (IV, i)*

*God give them wisdom that have it; and those that
are fools, let them use their talents ... Better a witty
fool than a foolish wit.*
> *Twelfth Night (I, v)*

> *Yet hath Sir Proteus ...*
*Made use and fair advantage of his days;
His years but young, but his experience old;
His head unmellow'd, but his judgment ripe...*
>> *Two Gentlemen of Verona (II, iv)*

WORK

Com: Take your choice of those
That best aid your action.
Mar: Those are they
That most are willing.
              Coriolanus (I, vi)

Action is eloquence...
              Coriolanus (III, ii)

    My endeavors
Have ever come too short of my desires...
              King Henry VIII (III, ii)

   His promises were ... mighty,
But his performance ... nothing.
              King Henry VIII (IV, ii)

                ... his noble hand
Did win what he did spend, and spent not that
Which his triumphant father's hand had won...
              King Richard II (II, i)

Awhile to work, and, after, holiday.
              King Richard II (III, i)

                    [forth...
Let him be but testimonied in his own bringings-
              Measure for Measure (III, ii)

No profit grows where is no pleasure ta'en.
              Taming of the Shrew (I, i)

Joy's soul lies in the doing.
              Troilus and Cressida (I, ii)

Now is my day's work done; I'll take good breath.
              Troilus and Cressida (V, viii)

NOTES

NOTES

NOTES

NOTES

NOTES

NOTES

NOTES

RETAIL ORDER FORM

"Shakespeare Ink"
P.O. Box 1451, Ogden, UT 84402

Please send _____ copy/copies of "Inspired Quotes from the Pen of Shakespeare". I have enclosed a check or money order for $10.95 (plus 68¢ tax within Utah) per book ordered. I have also added $1.25 per book to cover mailing costs. I understand I should allow 4-6 weeks for delivery.

SHIP TO:

Name_____

Address_____

City_____

State_____Zip_____

Area Code/Phone Number_____

Signature_____